DATA ADMINISTRATION

Data Administration

Simon Holloway

Data Dictionary Systems Ltd

Gower Technical Press

Published by
Gower Technical Press Ltd,
Gower House,
Croft Road,
Aldershot,
Hants GU11 3HR
England

Gower Publishing Company,
Old Post Road,
Brookfield,
Vermont 05036
U.S.A.

British Library Cataloguing in Publication Data

Holloway, Simon
  Data administration
  1. Data base management
  I. Title
005.74   QA76.9.D3

Library of Congress Cataloging in Publication Data

Holloway, Simon
Data administration/Simon Holloway.
P.CM.
Includes index.
1. Data base management. I. Title.
QA76.9.D3H65   1988   87–28913
005.74—DC19   CIP

ISBN 0–291–39765–4

Printed and bound in Great Britain by
Billing and Sons Limited, Worcester.

Contents

Appendices 123

Illustrations

Figures

Preface

This book has its origins, when in 1981 the British Computer Society Database Specialist Group set up a working party on the subject of data administration. It was my privilege to be the first chairman. The group was made up of practising data administrators, database administrators, and consultants in data management. Meetings were held on a monthly basis and at these meetings members discussed and argued points based on working papers. The chapter on tools and techniques is based on one of these working papers which I presented to the group; an edited earlier version of it is included in the working party's own publication. I gratefully acknowledge the contribution to my understanding of the subject of data administration by members of DAWP.

When in 1983, I joined Applied Data Research Ltd, I was asked to put together an education course on the subject of data administration. This led me to go past the areas under discussion at that time by DAWP. The comments that I received on the first runnings of the course led me to write a manual to accompany the training course and this is how the book was born. My aim for the book is to provide a simple guide to the concepts involved in data administration. This is an area, where there is little literature. Because we are dealing with a resource that is of prime importance to any organization, namely data, it is important that management as well as practising or prospective data administrators understand what is involved.

I wish to acknowledge the permission to reproduce and paraphrase from the following sources:

- John Wiley and Sons Ltd for permission to reprint and paraphrase from 'A Systematic Approach to the Definition of Data', C.R. Symons and P. Tijsma, *The Computer Journal*, vol. 25, no. 4, 1982.
- IBM United Kingdom Ltd for permission to reprint from *DB/DC Data Dictionary Planning and Design Textbook*, IBM SR20–74780, Sept. 1982 details on the 'OF' language and use of Standard Abbreviations.
- Dipak Ganguli of Applied Data Research Ltd for permission to reprint from 'Information Management using a Relational Database', British Computer Society Database Specialist Group, DATABASE 84 conference proceedings, *Database Design Update*, April 1984.
- Dipak Ganguli and Robert Hailstone of Applied Data Research Ltd,

my fellow authors, for permission to reprint from 'ADR ask "Throw it away?"', Xephon Consultancy Report, Prototyping Systems and Applications Productivity, Xephon Technology Transfer Ltd, November 1985.

My thanks are also given to Mrs Pamela Caffyn for the grand job she did in proof reading this book.

Simon Holloway
Hitchin

1

What is data administration?

1.1 Introduction

Those who work in the field of database are constantly being challenged both by the burgeoning nature of the field and by the rapidity of new developments. One of the new emerging areas is data administration; this refers to the management, planning and documentation of the data resource of a company.

The key concept in the move towards data administration has been that data, like people, money and materials should be treated as a critical resource that any company has to manage. Providing accurate, relevant and timely information entails a significant cost for a company and presents a substantial challenge.

Edelman[1] states that 'Information is the prime asset, second only to people'. I believe that everyone will agree that people are an organization's most important asset. Well just think how much more of an asset or how much more of a contribution these people could provide to the success of our organization, if we can supply them with meaningful, timely and accurate information with which to do their jobs. What is needed is effective information management to help us achieve corporate goals.

1.2 Setting the scene

When computers were first sold to commercial organizations, the buyers were convinced that here was the solution to all their data-processing problems. The computer would cope more than adequately with anticipated increases in volume, and would make possible the provision of more and timely management information. That was not to be the case, except in the few organizations that actually devoted considerable effort into getting the best use out of the computer.

Then in the late 1960s came database management systems. An almost carbon-copy situation occurred as for when computers were first introduced. Only if the organization spent considerable effort were returns gained.

Hard on the heels of database management systems came data dictionaries. Once again history repeated itself. The problem, said the data dictionary advocates, was not in the processing of the data, but in the recording of 'data about data' (referred to as *meta-data*). Many companies purchased or rented dictionary software, but let it fall into disuse. This happened for three reasons. Firstly, the dictionary was installed but used in the wrong context. Secondly, meta-data came to be seen simply as some more data vying for the attentions of an already stretched data-processing function. Lastly, the first dictionary software was not actively involved in the application development cycle, but took a passive role. The tool was there, misplaced and with no real commitment to its effective use.

1.3 The information age

Naisbitt[2] talks about the fact that two hundred years ago we were basically an agricultural society involved in the growing of food to feed ourselves. About the turn of the nineteenth century we evolved into an industrial society where the measure of success of an organization was how many goods and products could be produced by an assembly line or in a factory. We were involved in the industrial society until the late 1950s, when the introduction of the computer happened. With this, people realized that they could utilize information produced by the computer to achieve corporate success and growth. We then evolved into what is known today as the information society. Information is necessary for us to succeed in the 1980s and 1990s (see Figure 1.1).

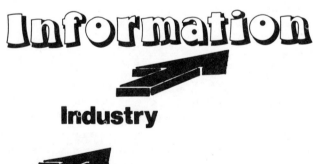

Figure 1.1 Information age

Data has always been part of human activity. In ancient civilizations its storage and interpretations were often in the hands of an élite body. In contrast, modern society has open proliferation of data, and the codes (the alphabet) are usually known to all. There are certain exceptions to this statement, when concealment is still practised.

Information has always been one of the main ingredients of the business processes and forms the basis for all decision-making; whether in a corporate or personal sense. Computers have had a profound effect on information and the manner in which it is transmitted, presented, assimilated and used for a given purpose.

Data and information are clearly distinguishable from each other. Data has definite form and has to be looked at in order that information can be obtained from it; this may or may not change the state of knowledge of an individual. Computers have added new dimensions of great significance. Firstly, the speed with which data can be communicated has been greatly increased. Thus the consequent speed in retrieval of information has been increased. Secondly the volume of data that can be handled is increased. These two factors have created an overwhelming change in the process of decision-making. There are two other major factors, namely accuracy and timeliness of data.

Data has to be regarded as a commodity that requires management in the same way as materials, money or people. There has to be a central store, so that items can be stored, located, retrieved, updated and transferred uniquely. In addition, the attributes associated with each item of data need to be collected. But to do this effectively, a company needs to invest resources in the use of 'data administration'.

1.4 Data administration

In the 1970s a certain degree of specialization in managing the data resource of a company emerged from the data-processing function, this specialization was called by two names:

- Data administration
- Database administration

In 1982, Nolan[3] published a report detailing the results of a survey that he had carried out. He identified that we develop three levels of information systems within our organizations, and that there are six stages of DP growth and maturity.

Data requirements at different management levels
Management levels can be categorized into three levels:

- Operational
- Functional

● General

Data to support these different levels are often different aggregates or combinations of the same detailed data (see Figure 1.2).

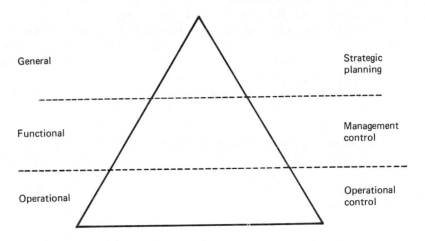

General

Strategic planning

Functional

Management control

Operational

Operational control

Figure 1.2   Management levels of data

The operational level needs very specific information for daily business activities. These are the systems that automate the basic business functions, such as accounts receivable, payroll inventory and so forth. Typically, when these systems were designed, the data to be used by these systems was also designed. So at the operational level there was a one-for-one relationship between the system and the data used by that system. DP used whatever was the most current state-of-the-art technology available for the creation of their data structures. This resulted in the data for one system being quite likely to look completely different from the data for another system. Consequently, when it came to use data from a different system, DP became involved in additional maintenance to solve the problem.

The management control level corresponds to the second line management or higher, and is concerned with summary information, historical data, quarterly information, year-to-date data, and so on. For example, I might have an accounting management control system. It would need data from all of the operational accounting systems such as, accounts receivable, accounts payable, payroll, billing, and so forth. However, since many of the various accounting applications might have different data structures, because they were developed over time, the data is not readily available to these management control systems. The data has to be programmed out.

Strategic planning is done at the upper levels of management and requires data to help with the setting of long-range policy and company direction. When systems are individually developed without concern for overall requirements, it is difficult to share data for these multiple needs.

To have a flexible information structure serve all system needs and levels of management, vertical and horizontal integration of data is necessary. The data required to satisfy these areas can be very different, depending upon the level you are trying to support. The ideal solution is to have data that can be shared by different operational areas. Using a strategic planning method allows a company to analyse its business requirements and develop a flexible information structure to support the needs of all management levels.

The six stages of DP growth and maturity

Nolan defined six stages of data processing (see Figure 1.3). Stage 1 was where the basic business functions were automated, and this was done to reduce costs and to make people more productive and more effective in accomplishing their jobs. This whole effort was being done with the minimum amount of planning and control. DP was delivering a useful service that helped to run organizations more efficiently. Because of this acceptance, the end users started to ask for more.

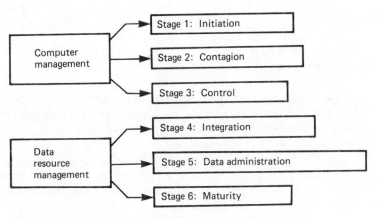

Figure 1.3   Nolan's six stages of data processing

In stage 2, a lot of systems were expanded and developed. Each system had a unique set of data to be processed. As a result, there were systems and data all over the organization, and this was done with even less planning and control. The results of stage 2 were chaos. Much of the information referenced by these systems and programs was redundant information, and it became very difficult to maintain currency. Finally at the end of stage 2, management became convinced that they needed time to take stock of the systems and information that was available.

Stage 3 was where existing applications were restructured to try to make use of the information that already existed. Information was passed from one system to the next. In stage 3, in order to accomplish this restructuring, some middle-management control systems had to be instituted. But something more important happened in stage 3. Until this point, the focus had been on the computer, the computer was the asset of the organization – the prime resource – the reason for being able to generate a lot of information for people. In getting into stage 3 and performing this restructuring operation, it was realized that it was not the computer which was the prime asset. It was the data stored on the computer, and this data could be very valuable to end users in accomplishing the running of the organization. Once it was recognized that data is the important asset, it became necessary to find a way to get your arms around this data to provide information to the various systems throughout the organization.

Stage 4 was where existing applications began to be restructured to use database technology. The goal here was to have one place in which to store corporate data. Instead of having multiple diverse architecture systems which required programming to access stored data, the information was stored in the database so that it could be readily available to everyone who needed it. In order to do this, some formal planning and control systems had to be instituted, and the end user was increasingly involved with helping with the information design and data definition.

Stage 5 says that all systems share a nucleus of data. Instead of having multiple technologies, architectures and multiple files which contain the same information, there is now one store medium for shared data to be used by all systems. Data administration will determine what information is to be captured, how it will be stored, who will have access to it, assign security, and so on.

In stage 6, all new applications which are developed, mirror the flow of the business. What does this mean? This is easiest explained by an example. Company A has a way of processing an order, company B has a way of processing an order, and they are different. The systems that are developed should flow with that ordering process. The reason being that these systems are easier to maintain, since a change to the ordering system would require modifying only that portion of the system requiring change. The systems would be easier to learn, since the end user is used to a certain processing flow, and the systems now reflect that flow. Finally, the top level of the information systems pyramid (the strategic planning level) can be addressed. This is because the data is now shared, and the information from the entire corporate structure is readily available to these strategic planning systems.

Nolan argued that stage 6 must be the goal of any organization. This was because the data resource was delivering useful, intelligent information to be used by people. To achieve this the data resource must be managed and controlled. How do I do this? The answer is simple: *data administration*.

What is data administration?

A number of observers (Kahn[4]; BCS DAWP[5]) have recognized that there is a distinction between the two functions of data administration and database administration.

Data administration is the corporate service which assists the provision of information systems by controlling and/or coordinating the definitions (format and characteristics) and usage of reliable and relevant data. Data that is internal to an organization can be controlled, whilst data from external sources (for example tax rates, independent marketing surveys), that is used by an organization can only be coordinated.

Database administration, on the other hand, provides technical support for data administration: performing database design and development, being reponsible for organizing and defining the logical view of data, providing education on database technology, and providing support to users in operational database related activities.

1.5 The scope of data administration

The scope of the data administration function must be as wide as is needed by a particular organization, in order to achieve the aims of cost-effective use of the data of the organization. A data administration function will always perform a service role, and will be involved in the identification and solution of the data aspects of the problems of the organization. Data administration does not directly control data, except data about the data of the organization and data about its own function.

In managing today's large and complex organizations, many of which are multi-nationals, and/or have grown through the acquisition of other established companies, it is seldom that the information required can be based solely on data under the direct control of the company concerned. Even in smaller organizations, the information requirements of senior management are more complex than before and require external data. In both cases, therefore it becomes a significant task to reconcile data collection from different areas within the same company, or data collected internally and externally. It is clear that to be useful, the scope of data administration must embrace all the data required to generate the information needs of management.

Some of this data will come from existing operational data processing systems, and should already be well-defined. Some will be held in local manual or increasingly micro-based systems, and will be understood locally but often will not be well documented. Yet more, and often some of the most important, will be gathered from outside the company. Business trends, economic forecasts, exchange rates and so on. It is important that the data administration function should not be limited to the relatively easy task of supporting the existing data-processing systems.

It is often right at the top of the company that problems of inconsistent definitions and inadequate data first become apparent, and support at this level is essential if these problems are to be tackled effectively. Once inconsistencies are enshrined in data-processing systems, it my never be possible to resolve them, and any such resolution will inevitably be expensive.

Data administration, according to DAWP [6], will primarily have a coordinating role, and will otherwise play a controlling role, related to the use of data. A more active role than this should only be adopted when necessary to advise, train, or coordinate to achieve specific longer-term goals. There are areas where guidelines need to be drawn. Outside these areas, data administration will rarely have authority or responsibility, but as a general rule, inside them data administration will be involved at a level that reflects the level of existing or potential data-related problems. Data administration is not responsible for actual data values of the data of the organization, but will be concerned with the meaning of the data.

The conclusion is therefore that data administration must concern itself with all the data which is of interest to the company, that is all the data on which management information is to be based. Within this context data administration must:

- Establish and promote common definitions of terms to improve understanding and aid communications.
- Supply a framework within which systems development may be planned.
- Identify gaps in the holding of data, and thus improve the quality and timeliness of information available to management.

1.6 The need for data administration

The need for Data Administration arises from the many problems that exist in collecting, holding and processing data in order to run a business operation and provide information to management. Some of these problems are:

- Management receives information too late for it to be useful.
- Management receives conflicting information from different sources within the organization.
- Internally-generated management information appears to be inconsistent with that available from outside sources.

- In a diverse organization, management can often not obtain consistent information about different parts of the business.
- Differences in definitions and procedures make it necessary to develop and maintain several data-processing systems which are fundamentally performing the same tasks.
- The availability of cheap data-processing power is leading to the development of small local systems which will in time become as expensive to maintain as their bigger brothers.
- Sharing of data between business functions is essential to the solution of some of these problems, and is impossible in the absence of any means of resolving conflicts and establishing priorities.

1.7 Cost justification of data administration

As organizations have become more competitive, to survive the increasing pressure of modern business, it is being seen that the providers of information have an increasing role in supporting the organization in the achievement of its aims. Systems are being developed to assist management in making decisions which have significant importance in the ability of the organization to run profitably, compete, or even to survive. There is also a quickening in the rate of change within all organizations. This need to change is often incompatible with the existence of large computer systems. A result is that in the vast majority of organizations, a constraining factor on the development of new business is the development time of new computer systems to support that business. Data administration must direct itself to assisting in the solution of such problems.

References

1 'Resources: A Challenge for American Business', F.Edelman, *MIS Quarterly*.
2 *Megatrends: Ten New Directions Transforming Our Lives*, J.Naisbitt, Macdonald & Co., London, 1982.
3 *Managing the Data Resource*, R.L.Nolan, West Publishing Company, 1982.
4 *Some Realities of Data Administration – a Management Briefing*, B.K. Kahn, Grad. School of Management, Boston University, Feb. 1983.
5 Internal working papers of the British Computer Society Database Specialist Group's Data Administration Working Party, 1982–1985.
6 *Data Administration for Business Organizations*, written and edited by members of the British Computer Society Database Specialist Group's Data Administration Working Party, edition 1, 1986.

2

Objectives of data administration

The data administration function has one specific role of advising management (DP, user, etc) on all data administration matters. In addition, the data administration function will normally be given responsibility for a number of specific data administration tasks.

2.1 Variation in responsibilities

The responsibilities of the data administrator will vary from company to company. The responsibilities will vary both in areas covered and the degree of responsibilities involved. Thus the data administrator may control, manage, advise, audit, plan, set standards – or any combination. It would be wrong and dangerous to try to specify a set of exact responsibilities that will suit all companies. The right set of responsibilities for the individual company will depend on the particular nature, business and history of the company. There are, however, certain factors that will strongly affect the responsibilities of the data administrator:

- Homogeneity or complexity of company structure.
- Company policy on centralization and decentralization.
- Use of database management system.
- System inconsistencies.
- Data protection legislation.
- Corporate business plans.

Homogeneity or complexity of company structure

The data administrator may be working in a company where there is a single DP department serving a cohesive set of similar users. Alternatively, he may be working in a company that is multi-functional, multi-site, or that controls a number of separate legal companies.

This will have a decisive influence on the nature of the company's data, the issues that occur and the work of the data administrator.

Company policy on centralization or decentralization

The policy on centralization varies from company to company, and may well change within a company. As with any other function, the responsibility of the data administrator will depend on the policy. In general, in a centralized company the data administrator will tend to control and run various data-related activities. In a decentralized company the data administrator will tend only to advise and liaise on those data activities.

Use of a database management system

If a company uses a database management system to control shared data, then there is a strong need to control the physical data. This involves a number of tasks including optimization of storage, data security and privacy, data recovery procedures for the database. These activities come under the heading of database administration, carried out by the database administrator. In a number of companies the database administrator reports directly to the data administrator. The database administrator may also have certain responsibilities for the definition of the data held on the database. In a non-database environment these responsibilities are likely to be dispersed round the DP organization (particularly in operations), with the data administrator tending to have only a general overview responsibility.

2.2 Responsibility of the data administrator

There are a number of areas in which the data administrator should have responsibilities assigned to him [1]. These break down into 13 major task areas:

- Identification of corporate information requirements
- Problems related to data
- Generating a corporate awareness of data
- Data definition
- Data dictionary control
- Data analysis
- Physical data models
- Impact assessment
- Data access
- Privacy, security and integrity
- Data duplication
- Data archiving
- Monitoring usage of data

Data administration policy

- To establish data management principles which determine the responsibilities of data administration, addressing the procedures and standards relating to each responsibility.

Corporate information requirements

- To determine and obtain acceptance of policies for the identification of corporate requirements.

Identification of corporate requirements will provide valuable input to application development planning. Identification of data requirements from corporate business plans can be input to a data modelling exercise to identify subject data areas. The aim is to develop a basis for an information systems strategy that takes account of current and future requirements of the organization, and will lead to the provision of better corporate information.

Corporate awareness of existence and value of data

- To educate the company on the importance of data and the problems of data, for example, inconsistent reporting of data caused by inconsistent data across systems and organization boundaries. A lack of understanding of real meaning of data can result in incorrect use of that data.
- To create an awareness of the value of data as a company asset, and to ensure the company is aware of the need to maintain the integrity of data held and hence its value to the company.
- To spread knowledge of what data exists and for what purpose data is used in all areas of the company, and to ensure the data is used in a consistent manner.

This responsibility is of fundamental importance as it drives many other aspects of data administration. There is, therefore, a need to gain the knowledge and then to make others aware that the knowledge is available. It is important to have a centre of expertise (that is, data administration) which can be approached for advice when necessary and to ensure everyone, including end-user departments, is aware that such a centre of expertise exists.

The first stage is to gain the knowledge and understanding of the data. The next stage is to provide an awareness of that data and to obtain rationalization of the different understandings held by different areas of the company into a common definition or understanding avoiding homonyms and synonyms. This will be an iterative process but should be the long-term goal of any organization. It is perhaps worthwhile initially concentrating on identification and rationalization of company or shared data (for example, customer data) as opposed to 'local' application-related data.

Data analysis

- To select the data analysis methods/techniques, together with the development of standards/procedures for use, and to integrate such methods/techniques into existing system-development methods within a company.

- To promote the use of and to provide an advisory centre for such techniques.
- To assist in the business analysis for the production of business data models and to monitor the consistency of results in different areas as these models are developed in more detail.

Data definition

- To establish standards for the definition of data, for example, status, naming conventions, aliases, owner of data.
- To establish the medium for the recording and communication of data definitions, for example, data dictionary.
- To define the level or extent of which the corporate data definition standards should be applied in the long and short term for each of mainframe, micros, local systems, global systems, specific areas of the company and so on, and to review such standards in the light of new methods.
- To establish enforcement procedures for data standards.
- To ensure a consistent approach across systems within a company by coordinating systems requirements for size and format of data items, coded values, and so on.

It may be necessary to implement data definition standards on a gradual basis to build up the level at which standards apply.

The level of commitment that a company gives to the enforcement of data standards and the size of a company (for example, number of systems) will influence the ability of data administration to perform quality assurance on data definition. The use of a data dictionary, for example, will provide assistance to the quality-assurance function.

Data administration is responsible for ensuring an awareness of the problems which may arise from the allocation of different codes to the same data item where it exists in different systems and for the necessity of allocating unique codes to key data items (for example, codes should not include a hierarchy of values which may change over time, codes should not be re-used over time, and so on).

Data duplication/data sharing

- To promote a policy for a single source of data.
- To encourage sharing of data across applications and to promote the creation of data that is independent of application.

Many of the problems of data which currently exist arise from the duplication of data held in the various systems in a company. This data will inevitably become inconsistent if more than one source of local updating of such data is performed and local meanings of such data develops. Although duplication of data may sometimes be justified (for example, for system performance reasons), it should be a conscious decision and not accidental. It is therefore the responsibility of data administration to ensure that any such duplication is essential and that where possible all duplicated data is originated from a single source.

By providing a corporate awareness of the existence of data, consistent definition and usage of data will enable the development of application-independent data.

Data dictionary control

- To establish the requirements for the use of a data dictionary for data administration and to coordinate the requirements of all other dictionary users.
- To select data dictionary software.
- To set rules and procedures for a data dictionary control function.
- To specify the rules for data dictionary use and to ensure the integrity, security and privacy of dictionary data.
- To monitor the use and content of the data dictionary to ensure compliance with established rules.

Data access

- To design and gain acceptance of access authorization rules.
- To arbitrate in disputes arising from requests for access to data.

With the growing spread of the use of data for purposes other than those for which it was originally gathered, there is a need to define access rules which state how a new user of a piece of data may obtain authorization to use it, and also to design procedures for obtaining copies of data for users who require data for use in their own applications. For example, who should be permitted to access payroll data, and who will authorise such access? It is a responsibility of data administration to design and gain acceptance of access authorization and copy management rules and procedures for a company and to see they are enforced.

It is important that change control procedures should include the involvement of data administration to ensure that any changes to access requirements are subject to authorization procedures.

Corporate data is data without which an organization cannot function. It is 'owned' by the organization. This data may be subject to external controls, such as national security policy or statutory requirements on personal privacy or the keeping of financial records. It may also be subject to internal controls, imposed by the organization itself and applying to its own departments or organizational levels, such as those arising from the need for commercial confidentiality.

Corporate data is usually shareable and readily accessible. It can be used for purposes other than those for which it was originally created.

It may therefore sometimes be necessary to restrict access to data.

Access authorization rules are a set of procedures for establishing which users are responsible for defining access rights to given items of data, and for handling new requests to access data.

The data administrator does not himself decide access rights. He coordinates user access requirements and where necessary holds negotiations. Occasionally an arbitrator may be necessary but this should normally be a committee of senior management and should only be the data administrator himself if he has a very considerable level of authority within the organization.

Access types

Access types may be summarized as: Create, alter, read and delete. Authorization rules must specify whether each of these is permitted to a given user for a given time. Data items can rarely be treated in isolation. Creation, deletion or alteration will frequently have consequences elsewhere and this must be anticipated by the data administrator. Conversely, it will often be possible to use the same access rules for a number of items.

It is important to take into account the nature of the access software. A transaction process which can read the value of one sale to one customer on one date is different from a management information system which can aggregate the value of all sales to all customers over the period of a year. Both could be described as read access to one data item but the information obtained is in one case trivial and in the other highly sensitive. This consideration applies particularly to copy management.

It is also important to allow for associability: access to certain data items may enable the derivation of other data which should not be accessible.

Responsible parties

Responsible parties are the users who define access rights for given data items. It will not necessarily be the case that there is only one user responsible for a given item or group of items; sometimes more than one year will share the responsibility. Suitable candidates are users who have defined the data: users who create new occurrences; users who can alter the data; and the users who benefit most from the existence of the data.

When the responsible parties have been determined, they should be identified as such in the central documentation (data dictionary) for the given item. The documentation is not complete without this. Responsible parties should be user departments or individuals identified by job title or organizational position, not their personal names.

This makes the documentation less vulnerable to personnel changes. Any changes in the structure of the organization must be reflected in the access rules documentation.

Access controls
Data Administration will need to specify (if not actually implement) requirements for user access profiles, that is, documentation of what access rights each user has. 'Users', in this context, includes systems development personnel.

Change control procedures should include, as obligatory, authorization requests for any change in access rights.

Authorization rules should also specify the action to be taken in the event of a violation or attempted violation of the rules.

In some environments it may be desirable for the users responsible for access rights to delegate authority to other users, or to allow those users to propagate their rights, as in the case of a manager being empowered to extend his rights to his subordinates.

It is necessary to consider the implication of remote processing, personal computing and outside services or bureaux. In each of these cases, data may be beyond the control of normal centralized access restrictions. It is the duty of the data administrator to ensure that the relevant responsible users are aware of the risks in these situations.

Privacy of data

- To implement and ensure compliance with aspects of the Data Protection Act.
- To establish the strategy for the specification of requirements for privacy of data

Within a company, access to data may be restricted to specified users. Data administration is responsible for monitoring system's design and production running to ensure such privacy is not violated.

The Data Protection Act is concerned with the storage and usage of personal data. Within an organization personnel will need to be nominated with responsibility for ensuring compliance with the Data Protection Act. Data administration can provide a service to assist in ensuring that legislation is not contravened.

The Data Protection Act should not have a profound effect on data administration but should reinforce a need for a competent data administration function within an organization.

The Act is concerned solely with the use of personal data relating to a living individual and which is processed automatically.

The Act requires an organization to register particulars of personal data with a data protection registrar. The information required may be summarized as follows:

- General description of personal data including how long that data is retained.
- Source of data.
- Purpose or purposes for which the data is held.
- Recipient.

Definition of data privacy
Data privacy within the Act may be defined as a disclosure of personal data to only those organizations referred to in a company's data protection registration particulars.

Assistance in initial registration
Data administration should be able to supply the company data protection officer with information to assist him with the initial registration. The type of information that could be supplied is as follows:

- Identification of data that relates to a living individual.
- The files that use that data.
- The applications that use that data.

The use of a data dictionary will greatly assist in locating the information described above.

Maintenance of registration particulars
Data administration should be in a position to supply the data protection officer with details of any new personal data to be held and the purpose for which that data is to be held. Data administration should also be able to notify the data protection officer of any changes in the purposes for which existing personal data is held.

Should data administration have the benefit of a data dictionary then the following information could be held:

- Details for registered and unregistered data could be kept on the dictionary and thus assist in keeping track of whether data has been examined or not.
- The dictionary could also be used in the holding of the registration particulars as supplied to the registrar.

Security and recovery of data

- To determine the strategy for data security and recovery.
- To ensure that requirements for data security and privacy are addressed in physical system design.
- To monitor production running to ensure the strategy for data security and recovery is followed.

Integrity of data

- To determine the strategy for data integrity.
- To ensure the requirements for data integrity are addressed during physical system design.
- To monitor production running to ensure the data integrity strategy is followed.

Data archiving

- To establish the strategy for data archiving.

There is much legislation as well as company requirements on the need to archive certain categories of data for various periods of time. It is the responsibility of Data administration to set standards to ensure that such archiving requirements are identified during analysis and implemented in accordance with the relevant requirements.

2.3 Responsibility of the database administrator

The database administrator is primarily responsible for the technical implementation of the database environment, the day-to-day operations of the database, and the policies governing its everyday use. The database administrator's responsibilities include:

- Establishing technical standards and guidelines: making sure that all the data is defined, organized, and represented in such a way that multiple uses and applications are allowed, and that end users, programmers, and analysts have specific, standard guidelines by which data may be input, updated, or accessed.
- Supporting policies and conventions of management: making sure that the users maintain the policies and conventions determined by management, including the data administrator, governing the use and evolution of the database.
- Reviewing application system candidates: determining whether existing application systems satisfy the needs of the users and conform to the design requirements of the database or whether they need to be modified before they are converted to the database system.
- Database design: analysing the needs of the users on a priority basis and employing the most cost-effective techniques for the design of the database to ensure that the immediate and future requirements of the users are met effectively.
- Control of the database environment: continuing monitoring and control of the database environment after the system is in full operation, including data dictionary maintenance, system additions or extensions, and documentation.

- Technical implementation of data integrity requirements: implementing the necessary data locks and restriction, conducting periodic security audits, supervising the authorization of access to specific data, and investigating all known security breaches to protect the integrity of the data in the database.
- Training for the database environment: holding responsibility for the education and training of the users in the principles and policies of database use which includes making current documentation available to the users.

The database administrator is a clearing house, a central agency for the collection, classification, and distribution of the information and skills necessary to the success and maximum benefit of the database system.

2.4 Database administration functions

The database administrator's primary functions lie in the areas of design, control and evolution.

Design

The database administrator designs the database to reflect the immediate needs of the users and accommodate their future needs. Some of the general responsibilities of the database administrator in the design of the database include the definition of the content and the organization of the database (data structure), the definition of the access to the database including the logical and physical reference paths and methods, and the allocation of physical storage in the database(s). The database design not only should reflect the users' needs at the time of the design, but it should also provide the means for incremental growth throughout its life-cycle to meet the future needs of the users. Therefore, the design effort is extremely important to the overall success of the database system.

Control

After the database system is in full operation, the database administrator initiates control techniques to ensure the consistent and effective performance of the system.

Through testing and acceptance procedures, the database administrator is satisfied that the design of the database is fulfilling the immediate requirements of the system, and that it is evolving properly to conform to the future requirements of the system. By monitoring the inputs and outputs of data through edit and validation rules, data checking, and access controls, the database administrator identifies any inconsistencies in data integrity.

The database administrator also reviews all existing application systems for their consistency with the data definition and usage standards, so the systems can be effectively converted to the database environment without major revisions. The database administrator makes sure that the development of new application systems effectively meet the users' requirements as well. The database administrator monitors the use of the database through access statistics and request/response statistics to ensure the maximum efficiency of the system.

Evolution

The database administrator determines the specifications and design of the extensions, services, and utilities for the database environment. The database administrator also documents the evolution of the environment via the data dictionary. The database administrator maintains the system development life-cycle and the procedures for security, privacy, integrity, and recovery. This helps to ensure that the system remains effective in meeting both the current and future needs of the users.

Reference

1 *Data Administration for Business Organizations*, written and edited by members of the British Computer Society Database Specialist Group's Data Administration Working Party, edition 1, 1986.

3
Organizational implications of data administration

The positions of the data administrator and the database administrator are relatively new to data-processing environments. Traditionally, their functions and responsibilities were handled by various people participating in individual projects or departments within the processing environment. However, the database environment makes it necessary to centralize control and management under one administrative group.

3.1 The problem

Data administration is primarily concerned with problems that cross company organizational boundaries. It follows that the relationship between data administration and the organizational structure is the crux of data administration.

Data administration is as concerned with the way the company is organized as it is with the data – someone with a mathematical bent might define data administration as the intersection of data and the organizational structure.

In order to have successful data administration – that is to have good data – a company must be prepared to pay the necessary price. This price is not so much in terms of money and resources, but in terms of organizational willingness to adapt, cooperate and spend time and effort helping to set up and carry out successful data administration.

There are companies where the different parts and functions are not prepared to cooperate with each other, where any issue crossing organizational boundaries is seized on purely as an opportunity for political in-fighting. There is virtually no chance of making data administration work in such companies. Attempts to set up data administration will fail, and can be of value solely in showing up this intrinsic weakness within the company.

3.2 Organizational considerations

An organization has various criteria to consider when deciding on where to place the data administrator and/or database administrator into its organizational structure to assure that the functions of the positions are effective. One step in determining the criteria is to analyse the existing organizational structure to assess the organization's current position relative to its size and its structure (centralized or decentralized).

Some additional organizational considerations in the establishment of the positions of data administrator and database administrator, concern their general responsibilities and relationships to the different areas of the company.

For example, the data administrator and database administrator responsibility directly impacts the information flow of the company. The decentralized control of a traditional data-processing environment is conducive to a very limited scope for the information flow within the company, usually confined inter-departmentally. The centralized control pulls the information flow outside separate departments.

Thus the data administrator and the database administrator have a major responsibility as the interfacers among operating departments. The data administrator interfaces with the end users concerning applications requirements and with management concerning systems phasing and information requirements. The database administrator interfaces with systems personnel in design approval, programming personnel in testing, and with computer operations personnel in monitoring the database performance. Security and recovery are also the responsibility of the database administrator in a database environment. Traditionally, these functions are the responsibility of the separate departments. Under the data administrator and the database administrator, they are centralized.

3.3 Evolution of functions

The installation of a database system in any traditional processing environment is a major project, and should be approached methodically to reap the maximum benefits. The data administrator's and the database administrator's functions may be approached as an evolutionary process as well.

Setting up the data administration function

The data administration function begins from two quite different situations. The first, and the less common, is when an organization decides at the highest level that data is a resource that has to be managed. The second is when one part of an organization at a lower level decides to take this step. Invariably it will be within data processing that this decision occurs. In either case the main role of data administration, is to bring about a change of attitude within the organization, to promote the understanding of data and to educate all members of the organization in the value of data as a corporate resource, and in the need to manage it effectively.

It may appear easier to achieve this when senior management is giving support, but the process of developing data administration will be the same in both cases. Firstly, data is used by everybody in the organization, but not everyone will be willing to entertain the idea that their management of it can be improved, or even if it needs managing at all. Secondly, data administration is concerned with making data consistent and shareable throughout the organization. This involves standardizing the way in which data is defined and used, reconciling discrepancies between different departments and systems, and establishing criteria by which the quality of the organization's data can be maintained and improved. These activities cut across existing organizational boundaries and can be seen to impose constraints, slow development and an encroachment on existing preserves. Therefore, it is recommended that the new data administration function begins by identifying a clear-cut data-related problem and sets about dealing with it. The business must be seen to derive demonstrable benefit from the technique of data administration.

Reporting position of the data administrator

This will depend on a number of factors, particularly on the structure of the company itself, and where the desire for data administration came from. The initial position of the data administrator is likely to depend on who wanted him in the first place. There are three main possibilities:

- From within the DP department (see Figure 3.1). In this case the data administrator should be in the DP department, reporting at the same level as the DP manager to the board. If he reports at a lower level, his ability to make recommendations across the different sections in the DP department will be seriously weakened.
- From outisde the DP department (see Figure 3.2). In this case the data administrator will, in the ideal situation, be on the board. Since much of his work will involve one or more departments, this will require considerable political skill to make it work successfully.
- As part of an important DP project (see Figure 3.3). In this case the data administrator will probably be a project manager reporting to the development manager – and after the project will then form an independent data administration section, reporting inside DP or outside.

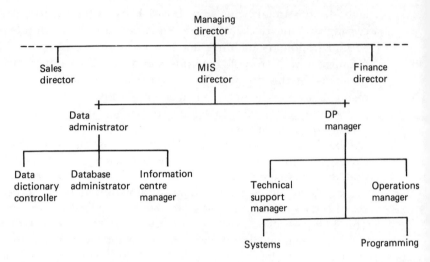

Figure 3.1   Management structure for data administration within DP

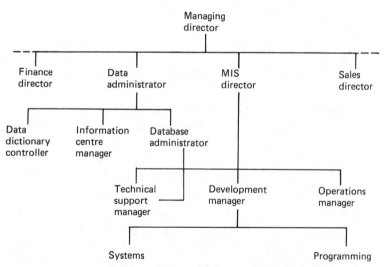

Figure 3.2   Management structure for data administration outside DP

Development of the data administration function

Having begun with demonstrating the benefits to be gained, data administration must move outwards to other areas, either by extending the same techniques to different parts of the organization, or by introducing further techniques. Eventually data administration must extend its influence right across the organization. The function does not need to be completely centralized and its structure should mirror

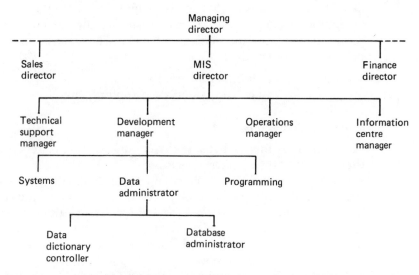

Figure 3.3 Management structure for data administration at project level

the structure of the organization as a whole. It will need to redevelop the data administration charter to set what its objectives should be for each planned period. In addition, it should be realized by the organization, that over time the data administration function could well evolve further up the company structure.

Relationship between the data administrator, database administrator and data dictionary manager

A number of data-related tasks may well be assigned to a database administrator. Furthermore, managing the data dictionary is only partially a data-related task. The important point is that the data administrator has the overall responsibility for advising on all data-related matters. If this is clearly recognized, then there need be no clash with managers who have data tasks such as a separate database administrator or data dictionary manager.

Use of committees

For many issues crossing organizational boundaries, it is not possible to have them decided by a single manager. Often there will be no common manager until the board is reached. Consequently, the only way that a decision can be achieved is by a committee (remembering that what the data administrator requires is access to authority, not the authority itself). If such a committee is to work, rather than become yet another debating forum, then it needs to be constituted and operated in a special way. First of all, the people sitting on the committee must be at the decision-making level – not the technical detail level. This means that any issue must be thoroughly researched before the meeting by the data administrator, and presented in terms comprehensible to the senior managers. The data administrator's presentation must cover:

- Assessment of the situation and the issue
- Choices and their consequences (including the choice of doing nothing)
- Recommendations

The committee then debates the issue, questioning or requiring further analysis – then makes a decision.

It is the responsibility of the committee individually to execute the decision and ensure that it takes place. The composition and coverage of such committees must vary as the data issues themselves vary. One of the major aspects of the data administrator's role as advïser to management on data matters is to recommend on the need for, the composition of, and the powers of such committees.

The use of committees either chaired by an individual manager (for example, DP manager) or between equals, itself provides the main avenue for the data administrator in providing advice on data matters to all relevant management in the company.

Skills and qualities needed in data administration

The data administration function can comprise one individual, a team, or a department, depending on its stage of development in the organization and the size of the organization. A full data administration function should contain three main areas:

- Managerial
- Promotional
- Technical

The managerial function exists to set strategy and to control and develop the resource of the data administration team. A good general appreciation of the business of the organization is essential, and so is an awareness of its policies. Promotional skills are essential. It will require tactful and determined promotion during its earliest years. Technical skills are necessary in such areas as data analysis, data modelling, data dictionaries and database management systems. There is one common skill involved in all three areas, and that is communication.

3.4 Distributed data processing environment

There may well be a number of data administrators working in different parts or functions of the company. How this works (that is, the extent of direct authority the central company data administrator has over the others) will depend on the general company policy on centralization.

In a distributed data-processing environment, data administration and database administration are fairly distinct functions. The network data administrator's responsibility is more conceptual, whereas the database administrator's responsibility is more technical.

Generally, data administration is a centralized function because it carries the responsibility for all the data of the organization. Database administration is generally a decentralized function because it concerns primarily technical implementation at the individual node level.

The types of organization structures that are different in a distributed data-processing environment from those in a traditional system are:

- Centralized data-processing facility with remote terminals
- Centralized and/or remote data-processing facilities with remote terminals including:
  1 computer operations at each site
  2 systems and/or programming either central or remote

Network data administrator
The major responsibilities of the network data administrator include:

- Network design
- Network standards (both data and system naming standards)
- Network growth
- Network management

The network data administrator is responsible for the quality and availability of the data throughout the network. Therefore, the network data administrator should be an integral part of the network design effort. The design definition, and control of all the databases in the network (from an overall administrative point of view) is the responsibility of the network data administrator. He develops and maintains network standards and plans for the addition of nodes and/ or databases within the network. The network data administrator also manages the use of all data.

The data administration function is based on the business needs and the data evolution plans for the entire network. Therefore, the network data administrator should approve any proposed changes to databases at any node. A change to any database in the network might affect the current or future operation of the entire distributed system.

Network database administrator
The following are the major responsibilities of the database administrator in a distributed system:

- Network coordination
- Application design and development
- Database management

Database administration is more technical than data administration. The database administration function should exist at every node which has the database management system. You can centralize the database administrator's functions if the job networking facilities are implemented as a part of the network to allow the central node database administrator to submit utility jobs and receive output from those jobs.

Essentially, the database administrator is responsible for technically implementing and maintaining, at each node, the standards and procedures developed by the network data administrator. The database administrator designs and manages the databases at a node to conform to the network data standards established by the network data administrator. He also supervises all applications design and development to assure network compatibility.

3.5 Administrative implementation

For many issues it is possible to sort them out through informal discussions at a working level. All too often the role of data administrator is based mainly on this. There is strong pressure on him not to raise major issues, and any failure to resolve, or more likely failure to patch over, such issues is seen as a failure on his part. However, it is not a failure. In any company there are fundamental data problems crossing organizational boundaries These are inherent in the data and the organization. Data administration can only address these problems if there is the necessary organizational procedure made available, and if management has the will to tackle such problems on both a data and an organizational basis.

The major steps to fully implement the functions of the data administrator and the database administrator are as follows:

- Establish responsibility/authority matrix
- Determine the present staff capabilities (skill matrix)
- Develop career path(s)
- Phase the time required for implementation
- Make contingency plan(s) for the functions

4

Tools and techniques for managing the data resource

4.1 Introduction

Ideally the techniques and tools available to Data Administration would enable the appropriate duties to be performed in such a way as to be:

- Effective
- Efficient
- Repeatable

What has been done in the software industry to help companies manage their data resource? There are six facilities that have been provided:

- Database management systems – to allow applications to share data.
- Data dictionary systems – to allow automated control and documentation of the data.
- CASE tools – to automate the analysis and design processes.
- Query languages – to allow end user access to data.
- Fourth-generation systems – to allow for more rapid application development.
- System development methodologies – to allow for planned development of data resource.

4.2 Database management systems

Traditionally, data files were designed to serve individual applications such as inventory control, payroll, accounts receivable, etc. Each data file was specially designed for its own application and stored separately in the computer. Often, the data files of different applications have contained common data fields. This redundant data has caused extra problems for the user because it has become difficult to keep consistency. Furthermore, the same data in different fields can have different formats. This variance has meant that application programs have been tailored to specific data organizations and physical devices. As a result, when changes to techniques or devices have been introduced, or new applications have been specified, the existing application programs have needed to be modified, thus adding to the cost of data processing.

These undesirable attributes of data files have been largely eliminated by the use of Database Management Systems. What is a database? A database is a collection of data which are shared and used for multiple purposes. Any one user does not perceive all of the types of data in the database, but only those that are needed for his or her job. Thus a database is not only shared by different users but is perceived differently by different users. James Martin [1] gives the following definition of a database:

> A database may be defined as a collection of interrelated data stored together without harmful or unnecessary redundancy to serve multiple applications; the data is stored so that it is independent of programs which use the data; a common and controlled approach is used in adding new data within the database. The data is structured so as to provide a foundation for future application development.

There are a number of ways of structuring the data that are used by database management systems:

- Hierarchical
- Network (CODASYL)
- Relational

Hierarchical

The earliest developed database management system packages extended the basic hierarchical structures first used in COBOL header/trailer records. With a hierarchy the records are linked together in a 'tree' structure with direct access being provided only to the 'root' master record. This is linked to a number of first-generation dependent records, any of which may be subsequently linked to a number of second-generation dependents and so on.

For many applications, the simple hierarchical approach is not adequate. One difficulty is the lack of direct access to dependent records, which results in time-consuming searching of whole sections of a database. A solution to this, adopted by IBM in IMS and DL/1, is to provide secondary indexes allowing direct retrieval of dependent records according to their content. Another difficulty is that while one hierarchical structure may suit most programs in a system, certain programs want to 'see' a different structure. To a certain degree, this can be coped with by using logical pointers (logical relationships) at application level, but in itself defeats the main object of having a database management system, that of sharing the data.

Network

More complex structuring of data is possible with this form of data organization. In a network structure, a record at one level can reference any number of component data items at a lower level. This provides for a more natural view of data than hierarchical whilst still structuring data. This form of organization was chosen by the CODASYL (Conference on Data Systems Languages) standards group and has been developed to varying degrees of completeness by a large number of vendors. Almost any data structure can be modelled on to a network database but the generality of the system results in greater complexity for the package as a whole. In particular, a greater degree of careful design and tuning is required from the database administrator (DBA), who must try to optimize the actual ordering of records in the disc blocks, as they make a great contribution to efficiency by determining the number of disc accesses for a given traversal of a given set.

The early database management systems suffer from three major failings. Firstly, the logical views of data they used were designed to be almost identical to the physical storage available at the time. Secondly, the importance of the 'ease of use' criteria were not realized. Lastly, instead of allowing easy growth or new uses of the data, the embedded pointer system made new data become less and less flexible over time.

Relational

At about the same time as the inverted list database management systems were being developed, some research work was being carried out at IBM San Jose by E.F. Codd[2] based on mathematical set theory and a proven practical approach to manual file design (normalization). The result was the concept of relational models, whose primary advantages are:

- A program's view of data is completely independent from the constraints of physical storage.
- Data is available, with proper controls, for many services.
- Data usage is more flexible over time.
- Data is easy to use.

Relational database management systems break away from the linked record approach to data organization. They, in fact, support the belief that it is not data that is structured but information, that is data when it is used. Relational data organizations are based on tables of data built along set theory lines and the close parallel between data storage and the mathematical approach leads to definite advantages, particularly in the design of query languages and the distribution of data.

In a relational database management system, all data is held in a number of two-dimensional tables, called relations. There can be any number of rows (record occurrences) or columns (fields) in these tables, and the order of columns is not important. Rows in different tables are related by having the same values of certain columns.

Aims of database management systems

The stated aims of database management systems can be summarized as follows:

- Data should be totally free from the constraints of any specific application that might use it.
- Data would be available only to those people or programs authorized to use it.
- Data would be in a maintainable form.
- Data would be stored securely.
- Data would be available, on demand to all requests that needed it while remaining optimally available and useful to all.
- Data would be subject to strict accountability and auditing procedures.

Ultimately, the whole of an organization's data would be held in a coherent, corporate database. Because of this, any errors in designing the data structure (or inflexibility to necessary additions to the structure) will have far-reaching effects on the organization – and on the future trust of the users within it towards the DP community. The principal aim of anyone involved in implementing a database, therefore, must be to ensure the stability of the data structure by employing well known and tried analysis techniques. Stability in this sense does not imply that the database structure will never change (that is rigidity, not stability), but that when changes need to be made the 'knock-on' effect on other parts of the structure or related applications is minimized.

4.3 Data dictionary systems

A data dictionary may be defined as a central repository of data about data. In a computer-based data dictionary this data about data (metadata) is stored in a dictionary database. The software which manages this database is called a data dictionary system (DDS).

Data dictionary systems are very useful and powerful tools for documenting and controlling both computer and manual systems and their usage of data. It is a tool to which systems design methods, programming tools, testing tools and management control aids should have to interface. The dictionary should be viewed not only as DP's database of its functions but as the company's database about the data it uses and usage it currently makes of that data.

The information held in the dictionary has complex relationships. This complexity requires the contents of the dictionary to be organized as a database. There are two approaches to the implementation of this dictionary database which divides data dictionary systems into two classes:

- Integrated dictionary systems – these use a database management system to implement the dictionary database. The database management system is used as the access method by the dictionary software.
- Stand-alone dictionary systems – these do not use a database management system which can also be used to implement an application database. They may use one or more operating system files to implement the dictionary database. Some effectively incorporate their own internal database management system, which is used only to manage the dictionary database.

For full benefits to be obtained from a dictionary system the information it contains must be complete, accurate and up-to-date. Consequently, a dictionary system should ideally support on-line access since the availability this provides encourages completeness, accuracy and timeliness.

A data dictionary database holds information about data and processes of interest to a company. Ideally it should only be necessary to define information to the computer system once. It is therefore preferable that other system software products should obtain any definitions that they require from the dictionary. For example, report writers, query languages and fourth generation systems should obtain data descriptions they need directly from the dictionary rather than requiring them to be explicitly defined by the user.

To gain full benefit from a data dictionary system in a database management system environment the dictionary must be active. This means that not only should it be a reference source (passive) but that it should be automatically self-maintained by a variety of interfaces to other pieces of software.

Data dictionary system vendors provide a default data structure for modelling the metadata. This default structure is suitable for describing the data and processes used by most companies. However, in certain cases this default structure is unsatisfactory. To cater for this the vendors have made their products 'extensible'. This allows the data structure of the dictionary to be tailored to suit the requirements of the customer. The degree of extensibility supported varies considerably from product to product.

As the dictionary holds descriptions of the corporate data resource it is essential that it supports a flexible reporting facility, which should be capable of producing a comprehensive range of batch and on-line reports, as well as supporting on-line ad-hoc queries.

Data dictionary systems can be used at all stages of the application life-cycle, in order to support application development and maintenance. However, there are now some very powerful development aids available and these can dramatically speed up and streamline the implementation stages of any project. One aid, application/program generators uses the dictionary definitions to generate most of the source code for a program/system, whilst others (fourth-generation systems) are effectively very powerful query, report and update systems which replace traditional languages with more powerful and flexible facilities.

4.4 CASE tools

There is a small but growing family of software tools that have been developed to automate the activities of system development methodologies. The tools currently fall into two basic categories:

- Mainframe-based
- PC-based

The former are the older and mainly deal with synthesizing logical data models in third normal form from a combination of any number of local views. These local views may be from input forms, clerical records, computer listings or file structures. Any redundancies or inconsistencies are highlighted. The output is a set of logical attributes and relationships. Very simple hard-copy graphical output can also be produced.

The PC-based CASE products are very recent additions to the armoury of tools. They combine existing computer-aided design technology with a data dictionary, allowing the creation of a set of graphics-based tools that allow not only interactive modelling, but also creation and maintenance of data dictionary objects. These tools are implemented on powerful work-stations using high-resolution colour graphics and a suitable human diagramming interface (commonly either a mouse or a light pen). The models and their associated data dictionary objects should not be stored in graphical or pseudo-graphical form. The tools should be able to store and recreate the models using only the data dictionary objects. This allows not only automatic diagramming, but also overview and subset diagrams to be created.

The UK government is sponsoring a programme for advanced information technology in which collaborative research efforts are encouraged through the efforts of the Alvey Directorate. Within this programme, a software engineering strategy has been defined, which identifies aids to automate development. These are described as IPSEs (Integrated Project Support Environments). IPSEs are designed to achieve benefits in terms of productivity gain, improved quality and control. This is done by providing an environment which supports the formal conduct and management of system development projects. A few of these products are just now becoming available on the market.

These products help the data administrator enforce corporate data standards throughout the design process by validating against a data dictionary. The data administrator can use the output as a corporate logical design standard. Once approved, a logical model can be turned over to the designer to be implemented.

4.5 Query languages

It is highly desirable that end users who cannot program should be able to query the database, extract from them information they need, generate reports and in some cases update the data. For this purpose a wide variety of query languages exist. Some are simple so that an unskilled user can compose a query. Some require more skill and training to use them. In order for a query language to be generally useable by a wide range of end users, Martin[3] states that it should follow these rules:

- The means of establishing contact with the computer and signing on should be simple, natural and obvious.
- The user should be required to know as little as possible in order to get started.
- The dialogue should completely avoid forcing the user to remember mnemonics.
- The dialogue should completely avoid forcing the user to remember formats or entry sequences.
- The dialogue should never put the user in a situation where he/she does not know what to do next.
- The dialogue should provide a simple, natural and obvious means for the user to recover from any mistake or surprise.
- The response times should be fast enough to avoid frustrating the user.

Most query languages are designed for interactive use at terminals. Some are designed for off-line use. A small number allow you to choose as appropriate to work on-line or off-line. The typical capabilities of a powerful query language are as follows:

- Access to data from remote terminals
- A security mechanism to allow different levels of access (read, update, delete, create) to different users.
- Report formatting capabilities.
- Computational ability.
- Data manipulation capabilities (sort, count, totalling)
- The ability to save data for future use.
- The ability to create user files for future use.

4.6 Fourth-generation systems

The term 'fourth-generation' is open to a wide variety of meanings – no two definitions ever have quite the same implications (the same can be said for most qualitative rather than quantitative terms – such as 'user-friendly'). Fourth-generation systems imply that all phases of application design and development are catered for, not just the coding phase, which is after all a relatively small proportion of the total effort involved in developing and maintaining a major application system. There is however one central theme common to all definitions of fourth-generation system, and that is significant improvements in productivity over conventional methods of writing application software.

David Gradwell[4] stated that when one starts to analyse the scope and range of the facilities of these products, a number of contrasts become apparent. He produced the following list:

- Whether the vendor markets a single product or a complete set of integrated products that cover more than just 'replacing COBOL'.
- Whether the product set allows you to build full-scale DP systems as well as small personal data systems. Many of the fourth-generation systems around now offer performance as good as COBOL or in some cases better. Only a few of the systems allow you to build batch as well as on-line systems using the same syntax.
- Whether the product set caters for a range of DP and end-user skill levels.
- Whether there is a full range of decision support facilities. It is desirable that there should be clear meaningful names for data, so that the end users can see and understand the data easily. The ability to produce graphic output and/or to be able to easily switch from the fourth-generation system to the query language and back, become important considerations.
- Whether the product set supports a structured approach to systems analysis and design. One or two of the products are based upon data dictionaries that will support the documentation of a particular systems analysis methodology. Other products support the description of the structure of the system being built.

- Whether the product set provides a flexible database system. More rapid application development requires flexible database management systems if it is to be a success; for there is little point in building a new system in a week if the database takes a month to design and code.
- Whether the product set provides and/or is well integrated with the normal office automation facilities (word processing, electronic mail and spread-sheets).

Fourth generation is often referred to – incorrectly – as 4GL (4th generation language). Fourth generation language is precisely what it says – a very high-level language for specifying processing requirements – the often heralded 'COBOL replacement'. True fourth generation implies that all phases of application design and development are catered for, not just the coding phase, which is, after all, a relatively small proportion of the total effort involved in developing and maintaining a major application system. A more appropriate abbreviation might be 4GE (4th Generation Environment); this term will be used throughout the rest of the document.

There is, however, one central theme common to all definitions of 4GE, and that is significant improvements in productivity over conventional methods of writing application software (again 'conventional methods' is open to different interpretations depending on the individual user site, but is generally taken to be a high-level language such as COBOL or PL/1 together with file handlers for either sequential file structures or network/hierarchical databases).

There appear to be two driving factors behind the requirements for 4GE:

- The high cost of developing new DP systems.
- The increasing backlog and lead times now common.

Of these two factors, the first is often overstated – while reduction in costs is always welcome, there seems to be little indication that users are no longer prepared to pay for a well conceived and implemented solution to business needs. Conversely, it is the inability of the DP profession to react quickly to changing requirements brought about by market pressures which is causing many users to attempt to implement stand-alone solutions, often based on unsuitable hardware and inflexible software packages.

The prime purpose of 4GE software must be to assist the DP community to respond to genuine user requirements in such a way as to make it unnecessary for a user to attempt to seek alternative solutions.

4.7 System development methodologies

Why is a good systems development methodology necessary? It lessens the risk of wasting resources, and thus money, on system development. A proven methodology means that the most effective way of doing things is defined in advance of the project, so that at all times there is a framework for development staff.

In addition, it increases the productivity of development staff. A good methodology does this in a number of ways:

- By providing a standard framework so that the developer does not have to reinvent the wheel for each project.
- Like a good kit of tools, it provides the right tools to enable each development task to be successfully completed.
- It allows effective review procedures so that errors and inconsistencies can be identified early.
- It acts as a productivity aid by reducing the amount of development documentation.

A good system development methodology improves the quality of the systems finally developed. It forces the developer to produce flexible systems that are adequately documented as they are developed. In addition, it allows the analyst to accurately identify the needs of the user, as well as allowing the user to verify easily that his needs have been taken care of.

A methodology provides a management window for reviewing project progress. At each stage management have a checklist for accessing which tasks should be completed and which deliverables are due.

Communications are improved as a methodology provides a communications base between all those concerned with system development:

- User and analyst
- Analyst and programmer
- Analysts and database administrator
- Data administrator and database administrator
- Staff and management
- Operations and the development team

Finally, it makes planning easier. If you cannot plan it, you cannot do it. A good methodology allows you to plan, monitor, correct and re-plan as the project progresses.

For a long time, one could say that what was offered by vendors was either based on system analysis skills or on the new skills of data analysis, the 1980s has seen the birth of the 'framework' approach, that use a variety of techniques covering the whole development life-cycle. In 1984, The Information Systems and Analysis Working Party of the BCS Database Specialist Group produced a *Journal of Development*[5] discussing this approach. All the methodologies that are part of this group have two ideas in common:

- Recognition of a strategic planning phase linked to the business plans of the company.
- The splitting of data analysis and functional analysis into separate phases.

Some of the newer methodologies also recognize the importance of prototyping as an aid to speed up design and gain user acceptance.

Some people still treat data analysis as a separate technique. However, data analysis has, in itself, many diverse techniques and these are used at various times during the application life-cycle. In addition, treating it in this way can be dangerous in terms of gaining acceptance among systems analysts, programmers and DP managers.

4.8 Other techniques

'Change control' is a technique used to monitor and control changes made to systems and also to data. The impact of the changes is analysed and reported. Monitoring is usually applied through the use of formal procedures or in some cases with the use of certain software automated. The disciplines applied are to ensure that change fits into existing standards and for compliance with user requirements.

Interviewing techniques are fundamental to the nature of data administration. It is important not only to plan the interview from the point of view of the information needed to be gathered – this seems to be the point everyone picks on; but also to understand the psychology of interviewing.

4.9 List of techniques per responsibility

Data administration policy

- Data administration charter
- Management role model

Corporate information requirements

- ADR/RISD
- CACI/D2S2
- IBM/Executive Information Planning
- IBM/Data Architecture
- IBM/Business Systems Planning
- Inforem/corporate information strategy
- ISCOL method
- JMA/Information Engineering
- LBMS/LEAP

Corporate awareness of existence and value of data

- ISCOL method
- Gane and Sarson/ISTP
- Use of query languages

Data analysis

- Bachman diagrams
- Baker (soft) box diagrams
- Binary model
- Canonical synthesis
- Entity life-cycle analysis
- Entity modelling
- Functional analysis
- Functional decomposition
- Interpreted predicate logic
- Normalization
- Prototyping
- Relational model

- Arthur Anderson/METHOD 1
- ADR/RISD
- BIS/MODUS
- CACI/D2S2
- CCA/ACM/PCM
- CCTA/SSADM
- DCE method
- Gane and Sarson/STRADIS
- IBM/SDM
- Inforem/system development methodology
- ISAC
- LBMS/LSDM
- MJSL/JSD
- Nijessens/IAM
- SYSDECO/SYSDOC
- Yourdon/SA–SD

Data definition

- IBM/data description language (the 'OF' language)
- Philips data classification system
- Standard abbreviations

Data duplication/data sharing

- Database management systems
- Data dictionaries

Data dictionary control

- Procedures, guidelines and standards

Data access

- Encryption
- Passwords
- File design
- Active data dictionaries
- Database management systems

Privacy of data

- Sensitivity analysis
- Risk analysis

Security and recovery of data

- Recovery analysis

Integrity of data

- Naming standards

Data archiving

4.10 List of software tools per responsibility

Data administration policy

Corporate Information Requirements

- Business 4S Technology/DAWN
- KnowledgeWare Inc/Information Planner
- LBMS/SUPER-MATE

Corporate awareness of existence and value of data

- ADR/DATAQUERY
- ICL/QUERYMASTER

Data analysis

- Analyst Workbench Products/DATA MODELLER
- Arthur Anderson/DESIGN–1
- BIS/IPSE
- CAP/FORTUNE

- Cincom/NORMAL
- Corex/CorVision
- Data Administration Inc/DATA-MAPPER
- Intech/EXCELLERATOR
- GEI/proMOD
- ICL/QuickBuild Workbench
- ISDOS/Structured Architect
- ISDOS/PSL/PSA
- JMA–Texas Instruments/Information Engineering Facility
- KnowledgeWare Inc/DATA DESIGNER
- LBMS/AUTO-MATE
- LBMS/DATA-MATE
- McDonnel Douglas/ProKit Workbench
- MJSL/PDF
- MSP/DESIGNMANAGER
- NASTEC/DesignAid
- NASTEC/CASE 2000
- Orr/Structure
- PA Computers & Telecommunications/TETRACH
- StructSoft/PCSA
- SYSCORP/MicroSTEP
- SYSDECO/SYSTEMATOR
- Vector International Ltd/EVERYMAN
- Visible Systems/Visible Analyst
- Arthur Young–KnowledgeWare Inc/Information Engineering Workbench
- Yourdon/Analyst & Designer Toolkit

Data definition

- ADR/DATADICTIONARY
- M. Bryce and Associates/IRM
- Cincom/SUPRA directory
- Cincom/ULTRA directory
- Cullinet/IDD
- Design Systems/SMS
- Haverly/SGD
- Honeywell/DD–DS
- IBM/data dictionary
- IBM/DB2 directory
- ICL/DDS
- MSP/DATAMANAGER
- Perkin-Elmer/DDS
- Software AG/PREDICT
- Sperry/DDS–1100
- Sligos PLS/BYBLOS

- Stainwright Consulting Services/SAXIOM
- TSI/Data Catalogue II
- UCC/10

Data duplication/data sharing

- ADR/DATACOM/DB
- ADR/DATADICTIONARY
- AMCOR/AMBASE
- CA/Universe
- Cincom/SUPRA and its directory
- Cincom/ULTRA and its directory
- Cincom/TOTAL
- CTL/DMS–8000
- CCA/MODEL–204
- Cullinet/IDMSR
- Cullinet/IDD
- Data Administration Inc/DATA–MAPPER
- Digital/DBMS–11
- Florida/DATA BOSS 2
- Henco/INFO
- Hewlett Packard/IMAGE 1000
- Honeywell/IDS II
- Honeywell/DM–IV
- IBM/DL–1
- IBM/IMS
- IBM/DB2
- ICL/IDMS
- ICL/DDS
- Infodata/INQUIRE
- MRI/System 2000
- Information Builders/FOCUS
- International Database System/SEED
- Logica/RAPPORT
- MDBS/dBase–III
- MRI/System 2000
- Norsk Data/SIBAS
- Oracle Corporation/ORACLE and its dictionary
- Perkin-Elmer/DMS and DDS
- Prime/DBMS
- Quodata/QDBMS
- Savant/MIMER and its directory
- Software AG/ADABAS
- Software AG/PREDICT
- Sperry/DMS–1100
- Sperry/DDS–1100

Data dictionary control

- ADR/DATADICTIONARY
- M. Bryce and Associates/IRM
- Cincom/SUPRA directory
- Cincom/ULTRA directory
- Cullinet/IDD
- Design Systems/SMS
- Haverly/SGD
- Honeywell/DD–DS
- IBM/Data Dictionary
- IBM/DB2 directory
- ICL/DDS
- MSP/DATAMANAGER
- Perkin-Elmer/DDS
- Software AG/PREDICT
- Sperry/DDS–1100
- Sligos PLS/BYBLOS
- Stainwright Consulting Services/SAXIOM
- TSI/Data Catalogue II
- UCC/10

Data access

- ADR/DATASECURE
- ADR/DATADICTIONARY
- ADR/DATACOM/DB design
- ADR/DATAQUERY
- ADR/IDEAL
- CCA/MODEL–204
- Cincom/SUPRA directory
- Cincom/ULTRA directory
- Cullinet/IDD
- IBM/DL–1
- IBM/IMS
- ICL/APPLICATION MASTER
- ICL/QUERYMASTER
- ICL/REPORTMASTER
- Perkin-Elmer/RQL

Privacy of data

- IBM/RACF
- SKK/ACF–II
- Topdata/TOP SECRET

Security and recovery of data

- DBMS recovery utilities
- IBM/RACF
- SKK/ACF–II
- Topdata/TOP SECRET
- Westinghouse/FDR

Integrity of data

- Database management systems

Data archiving

- Westinghouse/FDR
- DBMS utilities

References

1 *Managing the Data-Base Environment*, J. Martin, Prentice-Hall Inc., 1983.
2 'A Relational Model of Data for Large Shared Data Banks', E.F. Codd, *Communications of the ACM*, vol. 13, Pages 377–87, June 1970.
3 *An End-User's Guide to Data Base*, James Martin, Prentice-Hall Inc., 1981.
4 'What do We Need to Put in Place to Exploit Application Development Tools Effectively', D. Gradwell, *Database Bulletin*, May/June/July/August 1985, British Computer Society Database Specialist Group.
5 *Information Systems Design: A Flexible Framework*, edited by R. Maddison *et al.*, British Computer Society Database Specialist Group's Information Systems Analysis and Design Working Party, 1983–1984.

5

Data dictionaries as an administrative tool

In the design, control, and management of the data environment, the data dictionary is the data administrator's primary tool. It allows him to closely scrutinize and understand all the aspects of data. Because the data dictionary is such an important tool for the data administrator, this section discusses in detail some of the particulars that make it such a vital part of the data environment.

5.1 What is a data dictionary system?

A data dictionary system is a tool for storing and handling data definitions. This encompasses a large range of products, which may be used during one or more stages throughout the system development life-cycle, for documenting and using information about the structure, meaning and usage of data. This 'data about data' is often referred to as 'meta-data'.

There are great differences between the 'activity' of available data dictionary systems. Some are merely used for recording and subsequent enquiry, others are used as an integral part of the analysis, design, development and live running of systems. Some are based entirely around a particular database management system, and some are actually integrated into the application database itself. The latter are referred to as integrated data dictionaries.

For the maximum benefit to be gained from the use of a data dictionary system, it should ideally be used throughout the whole of the system development life-cycle. Very few data dictionary systems are currently designed to allow this, but many offer an 'extensibility' feature, which allows the user to tailor the facilities so that they more effectively match their own specific requirements.

The areas where a data dictionary system can be used include:

- Strategic data planning
- Business requirements analysis
- Logical design

- Physical design
- Transaction design
- User interface design
- Sizing, modelling and prototyping
- Program production and testing
- Operational running of applications
- Performance statistics, collection and evaluation
- Database tuning
- Maintenance, enhancement, restructuring of operational systems

5.2 The need for a data dictionary system

There is a growing need for a deep understanding of meta-data, supported by formal documentation. This can only be brought about by a recognition that the information used within a company deserves proper management, and the availability of tools to support the formal documentation required.

With the spread of computerized information systems, increasing use of communications techniques of all forms, legislation, and with a growing awareness of the possible impact of information technology, management are gradually realizing that their organization's data is an important corporate resource.

Data administration requires a large amount of data to be held about the data to be managed. This meta-data must be comprehensive, secure and easy to access.

Data processing needs to hold even greater volumes of meta-data. This will be data about computer systems, computer data structures and their interrelationships. As well as the requirement for access in a similar way to data administration, DP should have facilities to use the data definitions stored in the data dictionary directly within the computer system. This can be done by a number of methods, varying from generating source language copy libraries through to systems that access the data dictionary at run time.

The data dictionary is a productivity tool not only for data administration but also for all DP. The dictionary stores all the information about data, databases, programs, reports, panels, organizations, business functions and other projects details. It is therefore necessary that an appropriate data dictionary system is available, and that appropriate procedures be in place to make the dictionary useful to systems developers and to maintenance. For example, during the data collection and analysis phase of database design, the data dictionary can be used to generate the following:

- Data occurrence matrices – a map of data to physical files and a map of user views to reports and panels.

- Transaction matrix – a cross reference of transactions to data.
- Data relationship matrix – a determination of the frequency with which pieces of data are used together.

5.3 Management of the data resource

A company's data exists in its files, in desks, on forms passing between individuals and departments, in communications to and from other organizations and as a result of computations performed on other data. The orderly flow, and presentation of this data to interested parties forms the basis of the company's informations systems. These systems enable the company to function in a coordinated manner, and to interact effectively with its environment.

For the company to be as cost effective as possible, it must optimize the use of its data resource to ensure that the information systems fulfil its requirements as completely as possible. Management of this process is critical, and to be successful will need:

- Knowledge of what data exists and how it is used.
- Control over the coordination of modifications to data and process definitions.
- Involvement with all strategy decisions affecting new uses of data, or the ending of such uses and data types.

In most companies, there is no central coordinating body for the definition of the business data that exists. That is, there is no corporate view of the data resource. To gain control over the data resource, data administration must be responsible for the collection and storage of information about the business data. It can then begin to impose controls over the use of the data resource, and develop standards for the definition of data. This cannot be done without a data dictionary system.

In any company developing computer systems, control over data definitions is required. There may be a large number of applications, and their requirements for data may overlap a great deal. Manual documentation systems tend to be inadequate in all but the smallest installations, because of the need to maintain a large volume of information, and the difficulties in retrieving relevant information. When a large proportion of the data in an installation is used by more than one application, it becomes necessary to establish more formal, centralized control of data definitions and their usage. This is accomplished by the function of data administration. The database administrator must ensure that all applications are using the computer data correctly and that it is being properly maintained. In addition, the database administrator must advise on new applications using existing data and on new types of data to be used. All the information about data structures and their usage must be able to be provided to systems designers and implementors on request. In order to perform these functions the database administrator must be supported by a sophisticated data dictionary system containing all the necessary information about computer data systems, as well as the business data requirements.

5.4 Control of computerized information systems

Computerized information systems are rarely static in form, size or complexity, and may change for a variety of reasons:

- Normal development and growth of a company.
- Changes in company structure due to reorganization, merger or take-over.
- Changes in software environment, such as change of manufacturer, machine architecture or the introduction of a database management system.

The effectiveness of the information system will be impaired if it is not possible to incorporate the results of these changes quickly and smoothly. Management, therefore, is in need of some device to help them achieve the transition. A data dictionary system is ideally suited to this need since it can provide the following forms of support:

- It records all details of the current systems and therefore provides a baseline from which to plan changes.
- It can record details of all proposed changes and can report on any inconsistencies or gaps in these proposals.
- It can report on some of the major cost factors involved in implementing specific changes and from such information a cost-effective implementation sequence can be devised.

5.5 The use of a data dictionary system

The most frequent users of a data dictionary system will tend to be members of data processing, but any member of an organization may have a requirement to consult the dictionary directly, on specific areas of interest to them.

Use during the analysis phase
The data dictionary system will be used by both users and analysts while documenting the information gained from an information resource planning exercise or from a business analysis exercise. A data dictionary system should be able to hold the results of a high-level

strategic analysis, and of a detailed analysis of a particular area of the business.

This data must be presentable: to end users so that the results can be verified; to systems planners, so that a data strategy and/or a system development plan can be developed; and to systems designers to permit the development of computer systems to satisfy the documented business requirements.

Use during the systems design phase

The data dictionary system will be used by systems designers. Firstly, as a source for the business requirements specification, and secondly, to document the developing system design. A good data dictionary system will hold various 'options' during this design stage to allow the modelling of systems, the analysis of cost benefit, performance, sizing of alternatives, or even supporting the development of one or more prototype systems.

Use during systems implementation

There is obviously a hazy demarcation between system design and implementation when modelling and/or prototyping techniques are used, so I will refer in this sub-section to the programming and testing phases of a traditional systems-development life-cycle, there being no difference in the type of support required from the data dictionary system, but in the sequence of the use of the data dictionary system's facilities.

For program development, first of all the procedural and data specifications should be obtained from the dictionary. To ensure the minimum of duplication of the data definitions, it should then be used as the source, or even object of the code and data definitions.

A primitive method of supporting data definition sourcing is by generation of source language copy libraries for the compilation. An intermediate method is for the compiler to access the data dictionary system directly and pick up the data definitions from there. A dynamic data dictionary system will provide the data definitions directly at run time.

Use during operational running

This is an area neglected by the majority of data dictionary vendors. A dictionary should hold all information about the running of live systems, the interaction of jobs and sub-systems, their resource requirements, output distributions, run authorizations, maintenance responsibilities, and so on.

The data dictionary systems should be used both as a documentation source for systems programmers, operations and maintenance staff, but also as an active part of the job control system ensuring effective job scheduling. As few data dictionary systems are designed to cater for the operations department in any level of detail, this is perhaps another area where the extensibility option should be used to fulfil requirements.

5.6 Conclusion

The introduction of a data dictionary system will have an effect at many levels within a company. It will create new tasks, but in return it will reduce the effort required by such activities as documentation and auditing of systems. A data dictionary system will enable management to control data processing at all levels – from the top (data analysis and conceptual data modelling) to the bottom (implementation and physical design), and would provide an effective means of communicating data-processing requirements between user departments and data-processing sections.

6

Data administration roles in the database design process

Perhaps the most important way for the data administrator to control and manage the data resource of a company is through the design of its database systems. The data administration tasks during database design can be subdivided into three areas:

Preliminary tasks

- Selecting the database design methodology
- User requirements standards
- Database design
- Data naming standards
- Data dictionary collection model
- Training requirements
- Strategic data planning

Database design process

- Guides database design methodology
- Consulted on user requirements
- Uses data dictionary
- Reviews data naming standards
- Guides data collection process
- Conceptual design
- Logical design
- Physical design

Post database design

- Data conversion strategy
- Database design model
- Database file test environment
- Database development to live change control
- Database file maintenance

6.1 Database design methodology

It is the database design that provides the foundation for the integration of the corporate data resource residing in the computer. Data administration in conjunction with database administration is charged with designing an overall database structure that is stable in the long term but at the same time meets the requirements of component systems. In the absence of such centralized control of database design, each system would go on its way and data integration across application systems would be impossible. It is therefore a necessity for a data administrator to select a database design methodology that fits with the style of the company, and preferably one that integrates with an application life-cycle development methodology.

The data in the database can be structured in several ways to facilitate its most desirable flow. The recommended methods are 'top-down' or 'bottom-up'.

'Top-down' structure

The 'top-down' structure starts with the most obvious or the highest class of information and breaks down to define its components. There are several advantages to the 'top-down' approach of information structuring:

- Initially overviews the area of concern – by decomposing from the most obvious, the final requirement or the complete area is viewed first, and then the individual requirements are taken apart systematically.
- Filters extraneous information requirements – by taking a whole and separating it into its component parts, attention is focused on only those specific requirements being analysed. There is less guesswork involved in relating components to the whole.
- Enhances management involvement and commitment – by decomposing from the largely familiar to the specific, attention is focused on the overall view of which the management is more likely to be aware.

By performing a 'top-down' analysis, the data administrator is less likely to miss a requirement in the existing systems not immediately apparent.

'Bottom-up' structure

The 'bottom-up' approach to information structuring and designing begins at the lowest level of information and builds to the whole or final information requirement. There are several advantages to this approach:

- Makes it easier to determine the differences between the operating requirements and the strategic data requirements because the information requirements are more precise at the lowest level.

- Builds as opposed to tearing apart which allows the data administrator to control more effectively the final information requirements.
- Parallels implementation by building from the bottom up.

To determine the information structure and design the most efficient information flow in the database system, a combination of these two above approaches is highly recommended. The 'top-down' approach determines the requirements for the design and the implementation framework. The 'bottom-up' approach addresses the requirements on a lower level of information and provides greater detail for structuring the information.

6.2 User requirements

One of the objectives of the data administration function is to represent end users when it comes to negotiating systems requirements with systems development teams, and also arbitrating between end users. The data administration function should provide the forum where involved end users come together and discuss their problems, procedures and systems requirements so that their requests can be implemented in a uniform manner.

The database design and the associated system design reflect the quality of end users' functional requirements as defined by systems analysts. The requirements definition methodology appropriate for database systems is drastically different from those used for traditional systems. Database design calls for the definition of end-user data views (*user views*) in a very specific and quantitative fashion during the early stages of the design phase. The user interview process needs to be a highly organized method of enquiry to determine the specific requirements of the end users. It should be structured and carried out in such a way that the response on the end users can be properly interpreted and evaluated to accurately reflect their needs.

6.3 Data naming standards

The data administration staff work with the end users and DP to define each item of data in terms of its size, format usage, and name. All this information should be properly documented in the data dictionary so that it is available to all projects and end users. Chapter 7 deals with this in detail.

6.4 Training requirements

There are four main approaches to the training of staff in new methods. These are:

- To train them as they are working.
- To supply them with materials to read.
- To send them on an externally presented course.
- To organize an in-house course.

The number and skill of the people to be trained very much depends upon the methods to be implemented. Besides providing full training to the people responsible for given activity, it is worth also presenting a brief overview to those people who will interface with that activity. This is necessary because their participation is required at certain points and times. It also promotes communication and understanding among the people working on different activities. It is best to train staff as near as possible to the time when they will use the products or methods. It is surprising how quickly a course is forgotten if a participant returns to the work he was doing previously.

'On-the-job' training

Training 'on the job' works quite well in isolated cases. If all the project teams are already working, using new methods or products, and a new person begins work, it is quite possible to explain what to do for the tasks that individual is involved with. Reinforcement and problem solving can readily be supplied by colleagues. In the opposite case, when only one member of the project team has previous experience, it is extremely difficult and time-consuming for him to teach his colleagues. This approach is bound to lead to long development times for projects. It will probably also result in techniques being incorrectly applied and in some instances not used. It can be seen that it is essential to supply good training in order to obtain the stated benefits of the chosen method or software products, and that time and money spent on training will result in rapid introduction and acceptance.

Supplying reading material

The second approach, which is to supply reading material, is also unlikely to be very successful. Each team member has to be particularly interested in reading the material in order to make time to do it. As there are usually no case studies or written work to reinforce the literature, it is difficult to assess how the methods or software will work in practice. It is also likely that team members will interpret the same reading rather differently, and so arguments about techniques rather than applications can develop during the project. If, for any reason, no course is available, the best approach is for one team member to read the relevant material and then spend some time explaining it to the others. Various practical exercises can be done to ensure that the techniques or product usage will be applied in a consistent manner. The person responsible for educating the others should also be made responsible for drafting the initial standards/procedures/guidelines. These can then be tested during the initial project and revised if necessary.

External courses

The third method is to send the staff on an external course. The benefits of this are that it is professionally given and should ensure that staff gain a thorough training in the methods or software product both intellectually and practically. Another benefit of an external course is that it gives staff a chance to meet members of other installations, and ideas can be exchanged. The main problem in attending an external course is that it will not reflect any tailoring of methods or software, which may have been done for a particular company. In many instances this will not matter.

In-house courses

The final method is to organize an in-house course. This is normally the best way of training a number of staff. It means that the course can be tailored to meet the requirements of the particular company. Finally, it is easier to generate enthusiasm in the team if they attend one course and get used to applying new techniques or using new software. However, if you use this method and want to use an external training company, you must remember to lay down for their benefit the sort of changes to their standard courses to fit with your requirements.

Once the new methods or software have been used successfully on a number of projects, you must consider what to do about training the rest of your existing staff and also any new members of staff. The method selected will depend on the level of experience of the people and also on the software or method involved.

6.5 Information systems planning

Most people agree that some planning for information systems is essential. Many companies now have business strategy plans and it is important that these plans tie up with the information systems plans, so as to give maximum benefit to the company by enabling resources to be devoted to the most beneficial projects. The widest context of information systems planning embraces two broad aspects, which are:

- Business planning
- Systems planning

Since the objective of using the database approach is to achieve data integration, any major systems development effort could span three to five years. These database systems are not only complex in terms of their components and interrelationships with other systems, but also have to meet the changing needs of the end users. This means the systems development plan has to be compatible with the business plan of the company. The data administration function develops long-term functional requirements, which are translated into business information models. This model, in turn, is used to develop corporate data models and conceptual system models. Based on the overall pictures produced by different models, the data administration staff generate a system development plan in conjunction with end users and DP.

Business planning

Business planning involves setting the direction of an organization as a whole. It may result in the organization radically changing its way of doing business, or changing the levels of the business, the geographical areas covered or the products and services offered. Such decisions are obviously made at board level within the organization and become corporate objectives. These objectives have to be translated into key policy decisions. The aims of the business then need to be documented in such a way that the information needs of the organization can be identified.

Systems planning

Figure 6.1 shows a summary of the steps involved in this process. Broadly, the phase consists of, first reviewing the information systems requirements to determine what new systems need to be developed. Secondly, the technical shape of processing is reviewed. This deals with how the systems are to be processed and what techniques and software should be used. Finally, the resource implications of developing the systems in the plan, together with creating the technical environment, are assessed and matched against existing plans. A broad schedule with nominated priorities is then created.

6.6 Data collection process

To collect and analyse the information collected during end-user interviews, the data administrator needs to specify a methodology for the collection of information. The methodology may consist of forms, questionnaires, and so on, that organize the information as it is

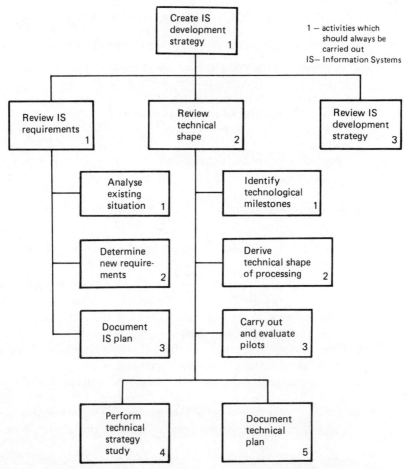

Figure 6.1 Summary of the information systems strategy phase

gathered. The information can be put into the data dictionary for collation and interpretation. A specific form for information collection allows individuals involved in database design to collect, review and collate information about any particular application. It also provides documentation of the data environment as the database design progresses. Outlined below is a particular approach to end-user interviews.

The first step in the user interview process is to select the individuals to be interviewed. The criteria applied in the selection are:

- Position
- Title
- Function

- Organizational entity (type and size)
- Geographical area

The next step in the process is to formulate an introduction to management and users informing them of the intention of the interview. The introduction should contain the following points:

- Statement of the objectives of the overall effort
- Description of the general long-term goals
- Objectives of the interview process
- General discussion of the database environment
- Description of the procedures to be followed in the interview including:
  1) appointments and schedules
  2) time required for the interview
  3) information to be gathered
- Request for cooperation

For the information to be useful in designing the database, it should be the right information. The following are classes of questions that yield the type of information necessary to do database design:

- *From which areas (systems) is information required?* A brief description of the data involved and an estimate of its volume.
- *What is done with the information once it is received?* A brief statement of the function of the systems.
- *What security precautions are taken with respect to the data?* A statement of access and data change authorization.
- *Are there any particularly sensitive data areas?* Data that could adversely impact the user if inadvertently or deliberately disclosed or destroyed.
- *To which areas (systems) is information sent?* A brief description of the information used by each system to determine data sharing requirements.
- *What are the realistic processing/response time constraints?* An estimate of the average and the maximum generic time response requirements.
- *Are there contemplated changes to any existing user requirements and/or procedures?* Changes to the application itself, not to changes in DP.
- *Are there requirements for the systems that have not been satisfied in the past?* Response times, access methods, change requests, etc.
- *What is the nature of any data sharing within a specific area (system) and between one area and others?* A brief description of the shared data and the various functions that use shared data.

6.7 Conceptual design

The conceptual model is the proposed mapping of the information gathered during the analysis of the existing information flow and structure into the database system. The definition of the conceptual model is the representation of the data in the database, independent of any database software. It is not constrained by the database management system, in that it is intended to simulate the real world as it exists at the time and describes record content and relationships between records.

One of the ways for the data administrator to test the soundness of the conceptual model is through access requirements tables which provide potential ways to organize data. The table identifies the process requirements of each transaction involving data in the database, such as:

- Data classes processed
- Frequency of occurrences
- Key(s) used in each process
- Volume of occurrences processed

6.8 Logical design

The logical design of the database is actually the mapping of the conceptual model to the database. The logical design may remain consistent with the existing design of the databases or it may be structured to reflect the desirable changes in the information flow. The security requirements for the data may impact the logical design of the database.

The data administrator and database administrator consider the following aspects when planning the logical design of the database:

- *Keys* – determine all the master keys and any secondary keys that can be identified from the user views.
- *Planned redundancy* – planning necessary redundancy by coding two or more records to satisfy divergent but coordinated views by relating records within the same file.
- *Processing mode* – determining the mode of handling for many-to-many relationships where key values in one file can lead to access in other files for specific information.
- *Relationships* – determining which relationships among or between data are recursive or cyclic and making the necessary physical provisions for that occurrence.

6.9 Physical design

The physical design of the database is actually the mapping of the logical design onto the physical processing environment. The physical design is dependent upon the particular database management being used. It must reflect the specifications for storage, access, and so on, that are established by the database management system. The data administrator and database administrator consider the following aspects when planning the physical database design:

- *Area mapping* – making sure there is proper grouping of logical files and resolution of conflicts within each grouping.
- *Native sequence* – determining the likelihood and frequency of sequential processing for certain records and providing the native key sequence to facilitate sequential processing.
- *Compression* – establishing the proper parameters and feedback for the compression.

In the physical design of the database, the considerations of the storage of data depends upon many variables such as:

- Recoverability
- Compression
- Device type
- Blocking factor
- Number of elements
- Number of keys
- Index padding
- Multi-user environment

6.10 Relational Information Systems Design (RISD)

In this methodology, the Relational Information System Design,[1,2,3] its terms of reference are taken from an information resource plan.
The reasons for this are as follows:

- The transition from an application-bound system to a central data repository supporting a large number of business functions, concurrently in batch or on-line, is a dramatic change. This change cannot be implemented successfully without a planned approach.
- From the start, the design process should be complemented by a data administration function. The latter, with the aid of a prescribed data dictionary captures the strategic database plan, the conceptual model, the logical model and the physical model for the database projects involved.
- The data dictionary should also support the applications developed using the databases. The data dictionary, with this in-built facility, should ensure synchronization across this whole arena.
- Management commitment is an important prerequisite to the success of the whole process by allowing for time and resources to undertake a sizeable task. The management also helps to define an extent of cooperation from the end-user departments.

The information resource plan

The information resource plan covers four major areas, namely:

- The organizational units of the enterprise.
- The functions within these units.
- The sources of data and information necessary to carry out the functions.
- The information entities. For example, person, places, things, and so on.

These components of the information resource plan are illustrated in Figure 6.2.

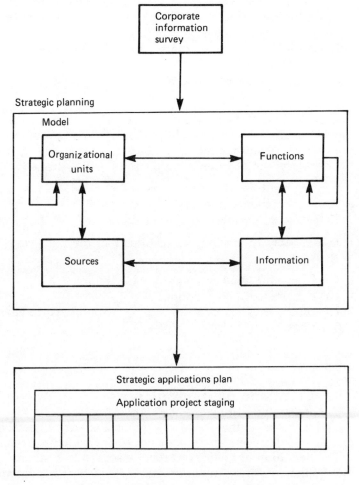

Figure 6.2 Information resource planning

The plan is refined by analysing the following components.

- Functional decomposition of the major functions identified in the plan. It produces:
  1) a breakdown of a major function into a number of major sub-functions.
  2) the areas of responsibility for each.
  3) analysis of the procedures for these major sub-functions.
  4) the definition of the management objectives that may influence the definition of these sub-functions or procedures in the future.
- The information sources by functions/sub-functions:
  1) identifying the source of information, for example, a document, a computer print-out, an on-line enquiry, a phone call and so on.
  2) a definition of flow of documents/information across the organizational units. These facts aid in the designing of the specification for integrating the database.
- The information entities:
  1) identify the major entities, attributes and events (top-down approach).
  2) concentrate on grouping these entities and relationships through the functions and sub-functions.

The model has all the ingredients necessary to represent the departments, their functions, the entities they use, the flow of information, the sources of information.

These facts can be recorded in the form of matrices, such as:

Functions/sub-functions vs entities
Source documents, and so on, vs entities
Department vs entities, and so on.

It is then easy to analyse the features that these matrices identify, such as:

- The cross-functional entities and their 'affinities'
- The cross-departmental entities
- The user-views of data as input, across departments, across functions.

These matrices help to decide on the strategy for integrating the database.

The strategic applications plan
This refers to the bottom of the picture in Figure 6.2.

The purpose of the plan is to define the subject databases and schedule their development with agreement from the management.

The definition of the subject databases results from analysing the facts gathered during the information resources plan described previously. The main components of this plan are:

- A high-level conceptual model (entity relationships, organizational units) of the enterprise.

- Identifying any corporate strategy that may influence the above model.
- Identifying the major database projects, their interrelationships, their order of priorities.

Figure 6.3 shows an overview of this top-down planning of data systems.

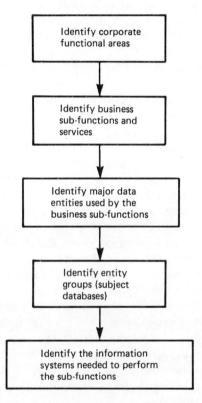

Figure 6.3 Overview of top-down planning of data systems

The subject database delineation is carried out as part of the strategic database plan. The process is refined by studying periodically:

- The high-level top-down entity model developed from the functional decomposition
- Analysing the entity/function matrix

The top-down process of identifying the organizational units, their functions, the major sub-functions, building the major entity model from these followed by identifying subject-database has a number of significant benefits. These are:

- The design is aimed at long-range management plans
- The design is based upon a clear understanding of the enterprise
- The design, therefore, should be:
  1) stable
  2) practical database integration through understanding of the functions rather than guesses from the entity model.
  3) the database projects can be developed through an agreed plan

The stage is concerned with the detailed development of any one project. Having decided the order in which these projects are to be developed, a bottom-up detailed analysis is carried out for the purpose of implementing the chosen database.

Prototyping with fourth-generation environment tools

Prototyping has been defined as the process of building and refining a working model of the final operational system during the development process. The main purpose of prototyping is to refine functions, inputs and outputs of the system during the design phase without having to wait for development to be completed. Prototyping is not a substitute for good analysis and design, nor is it an excuse to abandon proven structured design techniques, adequate documentation or good structured programming techniques. If used properly, prototyping can be an effective tool and an aid in developing systems that allow closer user participation in the design process, leading to systems that meet the needs of users.

In its simplest form a prototype can be nothing more than a mock-up of system outputs. Sample reports and panel layouts are developed and hard-copy representations are reviewed with the user. These will eventually become part of the detailed system specification. For this, almost any interactive programming tool that allows an analyst to design mock-ups interactively and then produce hard-copies, can be used.

A more elaborate form of prototype is a throwaway functional model of the proposed system. This type simulates the functionality of the proposed system. Users can actually sit at a terminal and use the system as it would be used in its final form. A limitation of this method is that it is still purely a model not capable of evolving into the final operational system. However, it is excellent for demonstrating the system and selling it to management. The prototype can serve as a useful requirements tool to communicate the systems specification to the application developers. For a throwaway functional model, any interactive software tool capable of simulating a real system is adequate, as long as it can produce a model fairly quickly. PC products are often used to produce these prototypes.

The third prototyping method, called an evolutionary system, has all the attributes of the throwaway with the additional capability of evolving into the final system. It is this method that RISD exploits.

Figure 6.4 shows the two main prototyping choices – the throwaway model and the evolutionary model approaches[4].

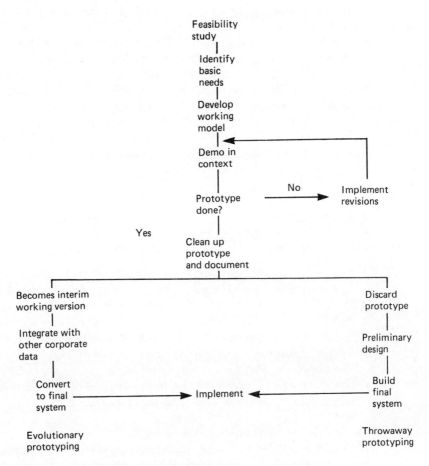

Figure 6.4 Forms of prototyping

Prototyping can be regarded in several different ways:

- A means of concentrating a user's ideas by presenting them back to him as they would appear when fully developed, but as part of an iterative cycle of refining the actual requirements.
- A means of automatically documenting a system as described by a user, and of gaining a user's commitment to stabilizing his requirements.
- A means of producing a 'cheap-and-cheerful' working system which can be rewritten for greater efficiency at a later date.

- A staged evolution of a system from initial concept to a complete, working, operational version.

Depending on the tools available, prototyping can be a mix of any or all of these views. The minimum requirements for accepting a system into the operational cycle of an organization should be that both the data structure and generated code conform to the site's standards and quality-assurance testing. An experienced DP professional who has worked within the organization for some time may well reach the stage where the output from his prototyping stage needs little refinement to meet the standards set. This is where the skill factor will continue to play an important role, despite the apparent 'deskilling' influence of fourth-generation environment.

Probably the most important role of prototyping is the process of defining user requirements by building and refining a working model, this should not, however, preclude the possibility of using all or part of this working model in the final developed system, provided that the various site standards are maintained.

Initial requirements

Before any prototoyping can be carried out, a minimum number of requirements must be fulfilled. These will include:

- Awareness of the software tools which are to be used, and an understanding of what they are or are not capable of achieving.
- From the information resource plan (or if this has not yet been completed, from the initial system requirements), the scope of the system to be implemented and an initial (simplified) data model.
- A table of sub-functions split into on-line updates, on-line retrieval, batch updates, standard reports, and on-line end-user facilities.
- The agreement of the end users to the method of progressing, and acceptance of the involvement required on their part.

Prototyping screens and inter-screen flow

About the one thing that most fourth-generation environment packages have in common is the ability to define on-line screens interactively, and display them back to an end user for refinement with editors of greater or lesser sophistication. Some more advanced packages permit a full facsimile of screens developed in this way, allowing the end user to actually enter values into the screens, with automatic validation of fields according to the specification. The user can thus see exactly how the finished system will appear at a very early stage in development.

Of more interest from the analysis point of view, this process gives us a definition of the local view of data as seen by the particular subfunction. This may not be complete at this stage, as validation of fields entered against an existing database table may be required, but at the minimum we are given a list of fields of interest, and part of the design process is to ensure that each field on each screen has an origin somewhere on the database, and is referenced in one or more places by other applications.

Having established the main update and enquiry screens to be used in the application, the flow between the screens also needs to be prototyped. This will normally involve defining one or more further screens which will be selection menus, and either writing or generating a simple program which will invoke the next screen in sequence or return to a previous screen. This also should be developed with assistance from the end user, and then the whole outward appearance of the application signed off by the user as confirmation that this is the way he wants the system to appear. This is simple to achieve provided that the software permits hard copies to be taken. Ultimately the control program compilation listing should show not only the logic by which control is passed between screens, but also include facsimile hard copies of each screen, with definitions of field editing and other relevant information.

During the prototyping process, whenever a particular part of the system has been agreed by the appropriate end users and 'signed off', that part of the developed system should be frozen by whatever mechanism the software tools make available – if necessary by moving the relevant parts into a read-only environment. This now becomes a part of the formal system specification.

Defining standard reports
Provided that the tools are available, standard reports can also be defined interactively, and either facsimiled or produced with the aid of a trivial program. The local dataviews from each report, as with those from the on-line system prototype, also need to be checked against the data available on the projected database.

Defining processing rules
Regardless of the type of language used within a particular fourth-generation environment software system, the same basic information needs to be defined for each application. The structure of a program will be determined by the nature of the data controlling it. In most batch update programs the driving force is a transaction file, which will be processed sequentially in its entirety unless an unexpected condition occurs. On-line systems are likewise normally driven by a screen input transaction which selects specific occurrences of entities (represented by dataviews). Standard reports and some on-line interrogation commands are driven by the database, where all the data meeting specified selection criteria are processed in a particular sequence. There are, therefore, two basic program shells, one representing a transaction-driven approach, the other a data-driven approach.

Having acquired a selection of data, various validations must be made before applying any updates to the database or presenting details to the report or screen handler.

Some fourth-generation environment systems take a rigid approach by providing fixed program shells which invoke user-coded routines to handle the exceptions. While this provides extremely fast generation of very simple procedures, more complicated requirements become progressively more difficult to fit into these shells. A less regimented non-procedural language, in addition to making complex procedures easier to cope with, may be used at an early stage to document the processing requirements of an application, later to be evolved into the actual operational program.

An example of a transaction-driven approach follows:

First attempt
```
<<NEW-ORDER>> PROCEDURE
    LOOP
        TRANSMIT ORDER-SCREEN           :DISPLAY ORDER-DETAIL SCREEN
            UNTIL ORDER-NO = 0          :USE ORDER NO 0 TO END RUN
        DO VALIDATE-CUSTOMER            :CHECK CUSTOMER EXISTS AND
                                        :IS WITHIN CREDIT LIMIT
        DO VALIDATE-PART                :CHECK VALID PART NO
        DO CHECK-STOCK                  :SEE IF PART IN STOCK
        IF NO-STOCK
            DO PLACE-FACTORY-ORDER      :RAISE WORKS ORDER ON MANUF. SYS
        ELSE
            DO STOCK-WITHDRAWAL         :DECREMENT STOCK COUNT
        ENDIF
        DO ORDER-ACKNOWLEDGE            :RAISE PAPERWORK FOR DISPATCH
    ENDLOOP
ENDPROCEDURE
```

This program structure, while capable of being compiled for example under ADR's IDEAL fourth-generation environment system, is equally suitable for presenting to an end user, and together with a hard copy of the appropriate screen will permit mistakes to be rectified while retaining full documentation of the requirements.

In this instance it would probably be pointed out that an order may consist of up to ten detail lines, and the functional description modified as follows:

Modified structure
```
<<NEW-ORDER>> PROCEDURE
    LOOP
        TRANSMIT ORDER-SCREEN           :DISPLAY ORDER-DETAIL SCREEN
            UNTIL ORDER-NO = 0          :USER ORDER NO 0 TO END RUN
        DO VALIDATE CUSTOMER            :CHECK CUSTOMER EXISTS AND
                                        :IS WITHIN CREDIT LIMIT
        DO PROCESS-ORDER-LINES          :HANDLE UP TO 10 LINES PER ORDER
        DO ORDER-ACKNOWLEDGE            :RAISE PAPERWORK FOR DISPATCH
    ENDLOOP
ENDPROCEDURE
```

```
<<PROCESS-ORDER-LINES>> PROCEDURE
    LOOP VARYING COUNT FROM 1 BY 1 UP THROUGH 10
                                    :THIS LOOP PROCESSES EACH LINE IN
                                    :TURN UNTIL EITHER NO MORE LINES
                                    :HAVE BEEN ENTERED OR 10 LINES
                                    :HAVE BEEN PROCESSED

        UNITL PART-NO (COUNT) = 0
        DO VALIDATE-PART            :CHECK VALID PART-NO
        DO CHECK-STOCK              :SEE IF PART IN STOCK
        IF NO-STOCK
            DO PLACE-FACTORY-ORDER  :RAISE WORKS-ORDER ON MANUF. SYS
        ELSE
            DO STOCK-WITHDRAWAL     :DECREMENT STOCK COUNT
        ENDIF
    ENDLOOP
ENDPROCEDURE
```

Once the basic shell of the program is acceptable to the user, each procedure named within it can be progressively expanded to accommodate all required validation, database updates, and reporting. By using this very structured pseudo-code an end user who understands his own system, but who would have no idea how to go about describing his requirements to a DP professional, can be driven progressively through the system design, and can contribute at each stage.

After each major change or addition to the specification, a new version (or copy) of the functional description should be started so as to provide a way to return to a known point if an error has been made.

Gradually the specification actually becomes the source code for the application, leaving only the lowest-level calculations and sub-routines to be coded.

As the user will have contributed to every stage of the development process there is little chance for misinterpretation of requirements to creep in, resulting not only in a system which performs in the way the user wants, but also a method which often highlights areas in which a user's own concept of the system fails to tie up with reality when demonstrated through a prototype.

At each stage in the design process, the system prototype should be demonstrated in its entirety to the appropriate users, and 'signed-off' as correct before starting any further phase. In order to make a more realistic presentation during the stages before the database design is completed, it is possible to code test data into the prototype programs in the form of working data (working storage in COBOL). The working data developed in this way as part of the prototyping approach has a double value, since it also serves to confirm the requirements of the local dataviews required by the program.

Bottom-up detail design

As shown in Figure 6.5, the detail design starts by analysing all the lowest-level sub-functions or user services within the organizational area covered by the sphere of the database. Each and every one of these services are the benefits that the end-users are going to derive from the database using various systems.

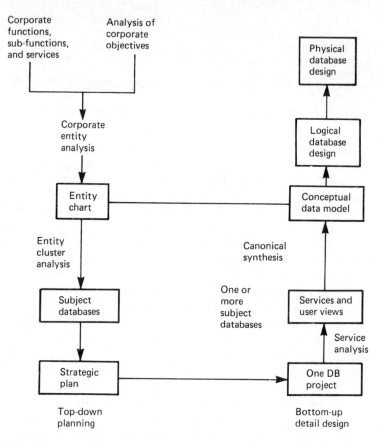

Figure 6.5   Top-down planning and bottom-up design

User service

User service has three components.

- The definitions of the user-views of data.
- The service delivery constraints with regard to response time, batch deadlines, security, audit-trail, reconciliations, and so on.
- The prerequisite and post-requisite services interactions plus the internal logic procedure of the service in question.

Note that a service does not only imply a physical output, it can also be a logical procedure or a combination of both. For example:

Calculate BALANCE.
If BALANCE positive

print DEBTORS-REPORT
Else move space to DEBTORS-CODE.

The above examples refer to a number of Data-Views, such as,

- the DEBTORS-REPORT
- the Data string that contains DEBTORS-CODE . . . etc.

The examples refer to a number of logical procedures, e.g.

- Calculating balance
- Creating the print record
- Update, and so on.

Figure 6.6 is an example of recording a service during the bottom-up analysis stage.

Service name: Book order report (BK—ORD)

Frequency: 1/week

Volume: 2000

Run mode: Batch

Output:

       Order number (ORD—NO)
       Membership number (M—NO)
       Member name (M—NAME)
       Member address (M—ADDR)
       Book number (BK—NO)
       Book name (BK—NAME)
       Book quantity (BK—QTY)
       Book price (BK—PRICE)
       Order date (ORD—DATE)

Figure 6.6   An example of the details of a user service

Conceptual database design
The conceptual database design, referred to in Figure 6.4 is developed through a three-stage process.

First stage
Collect all the user-views for every known lowest-level sub-function or service and pass them through the normalizing process by:

- Removing repeating groups – first normal form
- Removing partical key dependency – second normal form
- Removing transitive dependency – third normal form

The result is a large collection of tables that are in third normal form.

Second stage

Refer back to the top-down entity model from the planning stage and identify the entities that are within the span of the subject database in question.

On reviewing these entities, additional tables may be needed, and/ or additional fields may have to be added to some of the tables from the first stage.

Third stage

Process all the third normal form tables from the previous two stages using canonical synthesis to create the minimum set of tables that will satisfy all the requirements specification. The process of canonical synthesis can be automated using the computer; examples of this are DATA DESIGNER, DATA-MATE, DESIGNMANAGER. It outputs:

- The minimal set of third normal form tables that support all the user-views.
- The minimum number of relationships between the output tables that will support all the user-views.

The relationships are built as implied relationships on the principles of relational algebra through common attributes across tables. This final set of tables is the conceptual model of the database in question.

Using RISD, the most effective method of documenting the conceptual model is to use the data dictionary with appropriate CASE tool.

The logical design

One of the major benefits in this methodology is that it maintains a very clear distinction between the conceptual model and the logical model. That allows the methodology to be used with any type of data architecture (for example, hierarchical, network, inverted or relational).

The logical model is based on two types of information:

- The conceptual model of the database
- The 'data-views' to be processed by the various applications, some of which would act as input (for example, panels) or output (for example, reports, bills,) to and from the systems.

The mapping from the conceptual to logical model is a very simple process. The determination of the keys for a relational database management system, primary key, foreign key, alternate access key, are the only aspects that require some thought.

The simplicity of conceptual to logical mapping is clearly demonstrated in Figure 6.7. It is worth noting how easy it is to build logical relationships across tables without the use of any embedded pointer chains. The relationships are implemented through data values on common key/field combination across tables. There are a number of significant benefits to be derived from the relational approach to logical mapping:

- Because of its simplicity, it increases productivity.
- Because, the architecture is based on 3NF-tables the system is forgiving with regard to adding new tables.
- Because, the column order is of no significance, adding and changing new attribute fields to an existing table is a relatively simple process.
- Because, there are no embedded pointers to be built into the data, mass loading and database can be done in any order of the tables from sequential input, and the process is very fast.
- Because, the keys are defined in an index separate from the tables, adding new keys to create additional alternate access paths on the live database is a simple process. This helps to increase productivity during the design stage.
- Because, the relationships are implied, additional relationships can be created in the live database very simply. This is an extremely powerful feature to create additional data views almost unplanned.
- Taking all the above features together it is easier to see that the formal approach to the top-down planning and bottom-up detail design can be kept within resources and efforts that are practical and those the management can accept.

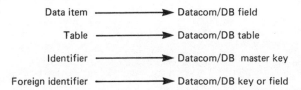

Figure 6.7 Simplified mapping from a conceptual to a logical model using ADR/DATACOM/DB as an example

If the system is to a large extent right rather than wrong, the database management system is flexible enough to cope with changes and improvements. This gives the project team a level of confidence that could not previously be deemed practical.

Physical design considerations
This is the final design step for any database management system before the database is ready for implementation. The required steps are highlighted and discussed very briefly.

Step 1
Name and identify the database uniquely from other possible databases.

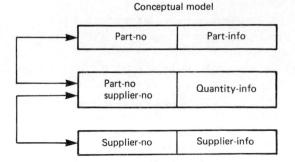

Conceptual model

Logical model

Part file

Datacom/DB fields	Part-no, part-info
Datacom/DB elements	Part no, part info
Datacom/DB key	Part no

Part and supplier file

Datacom/DB fields	Part-no, supplier-no Quantity info
Datacom/DB elements	Part-no, supplier-no, Quantity-info
Datacom/DB keys	Part-no/supplier-no, Supplier-no

Supplier file

Datacom/DB fields	Supplier-no, supplier-info
Datacom/DB elements	Supplier-no, supplier-info
Datacom/DB key	Supplier-no

Figure 6.8   Converting from a conceptual model to a logical model using ADR/DATACOM/DB as an example

Step 2
Identify and decide which conceptual tables are to be collated in one physical area. This would save I/O and improve performance.

Step 3
Identify and define access authorization for the various data views.

Step 4
Choice of keys

- Concatenated fields
- Exclusion of null values
- Use of synonyms

Step 5
File compression to save storage space.

Step 6
File logging and recovery using database management system logging and recovery features.

The database definition is generated from the data dictionary using the supplied utilities, or in any other appropriate manner depending on the database management system.

References

1 'RISD: A 4th Generation Development Methodology', Simon Holloway, Proceedings of Malayasian National Computer Society Conference, Kuala Lumpur, Nov. 1985.
2 *Information Management using a Relational Database*, Dipak Ganguli, Database Design Update, edited by G.J. Baker and S.R. Holloway, British Computer Society Database Specialist Group, 1984.
3 'ADR ask "Throw it away?"', Simon Holloway, Dipak Ganguli and Robert Hailstone, Prototyping Systems and Application Productivity, Xephon Consultancy Report, Xephon Technology Transfer Ltd, Nov. 1985.
4 *Shortcut to System Design*, A. Bernstein, Business Computer Systems, June 1985.

7

Data definition and naming conventions

7.1 The data administrators' role

Most authorities clearly state that the definition of data is a prime data administrator responsibility. Vitally important in this process is obtaining agreement on data definitions (meanings), representations, and structures. Although one standard may be judged superior to another, even superior standards will fail if there is not agreement on it by all parties.

A data dictionary can be used to store textual definitions of all data items. A text report can easily be generated, and should become the standard reference point for questions about any data definition. This is also an invaluable tool in training new employees, as they can be directed to read the text report in order to gain an understanding of the data they will be dealing with.

Agreement is the crucial thing. Even if the data is not right, that is, it is wrongly placed or unnecessary to an application, if there exists a common definition and agreement on that definition then resolution of the problem can take place.

It is not the purpose of the data administrator to force the designers to go through him in order to get anything done, but the data administrator can, by using a data dictionary and appropriate standards, cause consistent designs to be written at that site. To have consistent designs for both programs, application systems as well as data is a vital, basic goal of any enterprise, especially when a database management system is involved. Such designs are much easier to maintain. One of the biggest factors in the creation of consistent programs, systems and data is to have consistent naming standards. Everybody knows how COBOL is supposed to be self-documenting, and everybody also knows a bad COBOL program can be as hard to debug and maintain as a bad assembler program. Consistent naming conventions is one key to avoiding bad programs.

Another benefit of using the data dictionary to define data is consistency across application boundaries. Traditionally, different project teams would create documention in a format that seemed good to them at the time. The data administrator, by being a focal point of data and system definitions, can provide a consistent format which will benefit all.

To summarize, the data administrator's role in naming achieves the benefits listed below:

- Agreement on data
- Consistent programs/systems/data
- Consistent documentation

These can be achieved. However merely having the tools and the knowledge is not enough. It is up to the data administrator to create the standards and procedures that will produce the actual results.

7.2 Naming conventions

The primary purpose of naming conventions is to help users communicate effectively with each other and with the organization's systems. In addition, names should help in the managing of data dictionaries. They should be recognizable so that users understand what they mean, and they should be easy to use and capable of being derived simply. Ideally, a naming convention should be such that if different people attempt to name the same subject, they will arrive at the same name.

One of the major problems facing an analyst beginning to document new and existing systems in a data dictionary is the mass of different data elements with varying descriptions, derivations and other characteristics. Typical names assigned to data elements by users are brief, not very descriptive and clear only in the context of a specific application. Labels assigned by programmers are even more tense and are often incomprehensible. The same data element may have many forms of representation. To begin building a data dictionary, a consistent description convention would assist in defining the data elements, identifying redundancy and retrieval of data definitions without knowing user names or labels.

There must be a method of ensuring that a unique identifier can be assigned to every subject entered in the data dictionary. For many data dictionary entities, you will be able to adapt existing standards to the data dictionary naming structure. Other entities may not have any existing standards defined, and standards will have to be developed from scratch. Still other entities may have existing standards that are unsuitable for the data dictionary and must be changed.

The naming conventions developed must support multiple requirements, such as those for systems analysis and design, programming, database management systems, TP monitors, report generators, query languages and fourth-generation systems. In addition, in order to support the data dictionary, the names must have the following characteristics:

- Be recognizable
- Be documented
- Support communication among users
- Be easy to use and drive
- Be easy to control and enforce
- Assist in identifying data duplication
- Not be unduly application-oriented
- Support the peripheral requirements easily

It is also important to realize that the conventions will probably have significant impact on areas such as analysis and programming. It will take time to develop standards that have the agreement of all concerned. Some controversies are bound to arise, particularly in the programming area. The naming of *fields* is a subjective matter, and not everyone will agree with every proposed convention. The main thing, and probably the best that can be done, is to take time to develop a consensus in the organization.

7.3 Standardized abbreviations

This is a technique in which names are constructed from complete words or from unique, predefined keywords. Parts of the name are classified as shown in Figure 7.1.

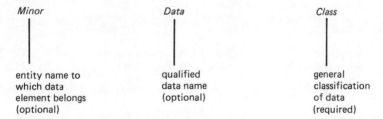

Minor	Data	Class
entity name to which data element belongs (optional)	qualified data name (optional)	general classification of data (required)

Figure 7.1 Abbreviation technique

Each of the portions shown could be abbreviated or used as complete words. The name is constructed in ascending order with specific terms on the left and general terms on the right.

Figure 7.2 shows two examples. In the first example, either 'customer' or the term 'abbreviated' could be chosen to be the most specific term, while 'name', being most general, terminates the designator. The second example deals with employee expenses. Expenses are an amount and have been chosen to be the most general term, while employee has been picked to be the most specific.

* Abbreviated customer name

    Customer-Abbreviated-Name (Cust-Abbr-Name)

      or

    Abbreviated-Customer-Name (Abbr-Cust-Name)

* Expenses in pounds claimed by employee at a specific
date and within a specific expense category

    Employee-Category-Date-Expenses
    (Emp-Cat-Date-Exp)

Figure 7.2   Using the abbreviation technique

It is important to standardize abbreviations throughout the whole
of the organization, in order to make the naming convention effective
and easy to use. A complete list should be derived and documented,

Name	Abbrev	Name	Abbrev
Account	ACCT	Indicator	IND
Address	ADDR	Inquiry	INQ
Adjustment	ADJ	Journal-Voucher	JV
Amount	AMT	Maintenance	MAINT
Automatic	AUTO	Medium	MED
Available	AVL	Message	MSG
Average	AVG	Modifier	MOD
Balance	BAL	Month	MO
Beginning	BEG	Month-End	EOM
Branch	BR	Number	NBR
Change	CHNG	Occurrence	OCCR
Closed	CLSD	Options	OPT
Company	CO	Payment	PMT
Contact	CONT	Percent	PCT
Continued	CONTD	Period	PRD
Control	CTL	Paid	PD
Corporation	CORP	Projected	PROJ
Credit	CR	Quantity	QTY
Customer	CUST	Quarter	QTR
Date	DT	Quarter-End	EOQ
Day	DAY	Reason	REAS
Debit	DR	Reference	REF
Define	DEFN	Segment	SEG
Delete	DELT	Serial	SER
Description	DESC	Services	SERV
Effective	EFF	Status	STAT
Employee	EMP	Terminal	TERM
Fiscal-Year	FY	Total	TOTAL
Fiscal-Year—End	FYE	Transactions	TRANS
Frequency	FREQ	Year	YR
General-Ledger	GL	Year-End	YE

Figure 7.3   Suggested abbreviations

and controlled and coordinated by one area. Each keyword should have only one meaning. Where ambiguity exists, a new keyword should be defined. Some books have been published that contain the standard and industry abbreviations. If a book is not available, simply generate a list of commonly used words in the organization and develop a standard abbreviation list with which the users feel comfortable.

Figure 7.3 shows some suggested abbreviations.

7.4 IBM Data Description Language – the 'OF' language

In the 'OF' language[1] names are constructed with the most general terms on the left and the more specific terms on the right, so the name ends up in descending sequence. Since the preposition 'OF' is used more often in designator construction with this technique, the language is called the 'OF' language.

Components of an 'OF' language designator are shown in Figure 7.4. It begins with a classword, which is most generally descriptive of the use of the data, followed by primewords and modifiers separated by connectors. Each of the terms must be highly derivable, easily understood, and arranged in a specific sequence. In general the grammar of the designator is hierarchical, placing the most general keyword first, then next most general and so on. For example consider the phrase:

'Abbreviated customer identifier'

The most general keyword is 'identifier'. Ask the question 'identifier of what'? Obviously the answer must be 'identifier of customer'. The next question is 'what about the identifier of customer'? It is 'abbreviated'. Therefore, the designator statement consists of these three keywords 'identifier, customer, abbreviated'.

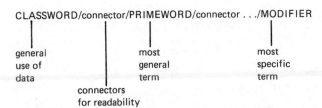

CLASSWORD/connector/PRIMEWORD/connector . . ./MODIFIER

general
use of
data

connectors
for readability

most
general
term

most
specific
term

Figure 7.4 General format of an 'OF' language name

However, there is an ambiguity in this order. It is not obvious except by thinking about the meaning of combinations of the words whether we have an abbreviated identifier or an abbreviated customer.

Symbol	Classword	Definition	Example
N	*Name*	Alphabetic data which identifies specific entities	Customer name Supplier name
#	*Number*	Alphanumeric data which identifies specific entities	Order number Part number
C	*Code*	Data which identifies classifications of entities	Shipment status Unit of measure
Q	*Count (quantity)*	The number or quantity (including fractions) of anything except monetary amounts	Quantity ordered Quantity received
£	*Amount*	The quantity of monetary amounts	Unit price Amount paid
D	*Date*	Actual calendar date	Date order placed Promised delivery date
T	*Text*	Data having relatively undefined content	Item description Shipping instructions
F	*Flag*	A code expressed as a bit and limited to 2 conditions	Deleted record flag
X	*Control*	Information used for control of other information during processing	Card code Transaction code
K	*Constant*	Data which does not change value from 1 transaction to another	Column headings Print masks
%	*Percent*	Ratios between other data values expressed as a percentage	Percent of shipments on time
A	*Address*	Subset of text	Customer address

Figure 7.5   'OF' language classwords

To remove this ambiguity we have a rule that adjectives follow immediately after the noun which they qualify. Thus the proper designator sequence is:

'Identifier, abbreviated, customer'

Since this organization is not particularly readable in this form, several connectors are inserted to complete the designator as follows:

IDENTIFIER (which is) ABBREVIATED (of) CUSTOMER

Figure 7.5 shows the 'OF' language classwords that are used to give general use of the data.

The overall language includes connectors used to make the designators more readable and 'class words' identifying the general type or use of data. In practice, these connectors are coded with specific symbols to reduce the number of characters to be coded, punched and entered into the system.

There are six connectors which may be used to structure designators to make them readable (see Figure 7.6).

Of	Or
Which is/are	And
Hyphen	By/Per/Within

Figure 7.6 'OF' language connectors

The symbols for these connectors are shown in Figure 7.7.

Symbol	Definition
.	Full stop (period) between keywords designators 'of'
*	An asterisk designator 'which is' or 'which are' depending on whether the preceding keyword is singular or plural
—	A hyphen causes two or more keywords to become a single word, compound word or phrase
:	A colon designates 'or'
&	An ampersand designates 'and'
/	An oblique designates 'by', 'per', or 'within'

Figure 7.7 'OF' language connector symbols

Examples

IDENTIFIER . CUSTOMER
IDENTIFIER (of) CUSTOMER

IDENTIFIER * ABBREVIATED . CUSTOMER
IDENTIFIER (which is) ABBREVIATED (of) CUSTOMER

IDENTIFIER . SHIPMENT * EARLY : LATE
IDENTIFIER (of) SHIPMENT (which is) EARLY (or) LATE

AMOUNT. EXPENSE * TRAVEL & LIVING
AMOUNT (of) EXPENSE (which is) TRAVEL (and) LIVING

7.5 Philips naming methodology

In methods and standards for the exchange of information, whether via transmissions over data communications networks or via shared databases, relatively little attention has been given to methods for exactly defining the meaning of the information being exchanged. In complex information systems, it is important to define the un-ambiguous meaning of data elements out of the context of particular messages, database records, or applications in which they currently appear.

To help solve these problems a methodology for formal definition of data elements using standardized terminology was developed within NV Philips Gloeilampenfabrieken, Eindhoven[2]. The method is com-plementary to present-day naming of data items, is based on sound theory of data analysis and can be used to define data elements both in intercompany messages as well as in local systems and databases.

Philips found that the 'OF' Language, although better than an arbitrary approach to data definition, has only a few rules for definition content. An international study of the contents and the use of several data dictionaries/directories in various DP departments of NV Philips Gloeilampenfabrieken was set up and found incomplete, misleadling and inaccurate definitions of data.

A methodology was devised with the goals to set up rules for correctly defining data. It is now an integral part of data and system analysis and design at the level of the conceptual model.

The first thing that was done was to differentiate logical from physical data by referring to the former as 'data elements' and the latter as 'fields'.

- A data element is defined as a basic unit of data which has a name, a definition, and a set of values for representing particular facts.
- A field may be defined as merely a named space reserved in a specific location of program or record for data values.

The data administration function in controlling the use of the significant data elements of the enterprise needs to know in which fields they appear. Perhaps in most cases there is a one-to-one correspondence between a data element in a controlled library, and a particular field. But there is often a one-to-many correspondence (see Figure 7.8).

When an analyst defines a field, he instinctively relates the field to its immediate context or environment. In principle, however, the definition of data element should not include any system-contextual or usage information. (The data element is only bounded by the

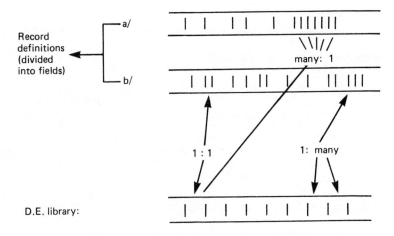

Record
definitions
(divided
into fields)

a/

many: 1

b/

1 : 1

1: many

D.E. library:

Field definitions may include complex rules about which
D.E. values may be included. For example,

Concatenation of values

Choice of values

Key-to (record id)
Attribute-of
Depending-on . . . (another)
Determining . . . value(s)

Figure 7.8   Field/data element relations

context of the enterprise.) Data element definitions may be valid for
centuries in a particular enterprise, but field definitions may change
with each system rewrite.

A field and a data element may be viewed as different levels of
abstraction or generalizations of the same basic idea (set of data), but
practical experience has convinced Philips of the value of drawing a
distinction. Figure 7.9 shows a list of the distinctions which can
usefully be made.

The method of analysing, defining and controlling enterprise data
elements has three components:

- A type classification system for enterprise data elements.
- Syntax rules for the structure and completeness of formal definitions.
- Use of a controlled vocabulary of permitted terms for formal
  definitions.

The type classification method
Classifying enterprise data elements is an aid to control and definition
tasks, not an end in itself. When they are sorted into smaller classes
the task of searching for a required data element is easier. Also,
analysing the definitions of all data elements in a given class brings

Characteristics	Field (type) (a named space reserved for data values)	Data elements (type) (a set of data values)
Identification	— a significant context-dependent 'user name' for example, think of proforma field headings — a symbolic name (code) for programming, unique within program.	— 'user name' has little use. — coded identification unique within enterprise.
Definition	— determines scope and meaning of contents, and all 'spatial character-istics' (see below). — always relates contents to those of other fields or records and the subjects they represent.	— determines scope and meaning of contents, and 'own spatial character-istics' (see below). — may relate subject-concepts to one or more other concepts regardless of how those other concepts are represented or stored.
Spatial characteristics own Relative	— defined length. — defined format, appropriate to programming language. — defined position in record, program and so on.	— length can only be determined if the rep-resentation is agreed — character type implied from representation. — positions are 'where' used' information and so on.
Contents	— empty, or a part of one or more values of one or more data elements per field occurrence.	— the set of values accord-ing to the definition.
EDP usage	— external schemas, record layouts.	— conceptual schema information modelling.

Figure 7.9   Field versus data elements

out the common features, and thus helps the definition process. The standard type classification method used for Philips enterprise data elements is based on the principle of sorting them according to the type of information provided by their values. (Compare the 'OF' language classification which is based on the type of value. That is, there are classes for data elements whose values are codes, names, counts, amounts, and so on.)

The Philips classification system has grown empirically into a three-level system of main classes, classes and types. Experience in training workshops and in practice show that it meets the above retrieval success-rate objective.

At the highest level, enterprise data elements are divided into those whose values give qualitative data and those which give quantitative data.

Let us examine the first group in detail, leaving aside the latter (also referred to as measures) for the time being.

The main class of data elements whose values give qualitative data, is known as 'main class A identifiers'.

Identifiers are data elements whose values uniquely identify or help identify certain objects or subject-concepts, or classes thereof regardless of the roles played by those concepts.

The main class for identifiers is broken down into nine Classes and further into Types, depending on sub-groupings of subject-concepts. The subject-concepts referred to are grouped at class level as shown overleaf:

- Points or areas in geographical 'space' (countries, districts, ports, addresses)
- Points or areas in organizational 'space' (organizations, departments, functionaries, networks)
- Points or extents of 'time' (periods, dates, times of day)
- Individual persons (employees, pensioners)
- Products and the 'resources' that are necessary for the manufacture (machines, tools), transport (lorries, containers, ships) and packaging of products
- Information units (transactions, orders, files) and the 'resources' that are necessary for the storage of information (volumes, media)
- Units of measure and currencies
- Accounts, projects, activities and such like
- Miscellaneous. For example, purely abstract concepts such as colour and language.

The following illustrate some classes of main classes given by value of identifier data elements:

- *Main class 4* – Sex or grade of person
- *Main class 5* – Make-or-buy class inspection procedure stock-booking procedure
- *Main class 6* – Urgency-class processing status

Such classes of subject-concepts are formed by selection on either:

- Permanent or temporary properties of the subject-concepts concerned
- Rules relating to the handling of the subject-concepts
- Rules relating to processing information about subject concepts in some way.

Such properties or rules must apply exclusively to the object-types of the type-class concerned. For example, 'make-or-buy-class' is a property of object-types such as 'product', but not of object-types such as 'person' or 'order'.

Let us next look at data elements whose values give quantitative data about the subject-concepts referred to by identifiers. They are also known as 'measures', and are divided at the highest level into five main classes:

M – Amounts (i.e. Financial amounts)
P – Prices and Tariffs
Q – Quantities (including lengths, weights)
R – Ratios, Percentages, Indices, Factors
T – Times

Each of the above main classes may be split, if relevant, into four classes:

- Measures of 'situations' (quantities of stocks, amounts of assets)
- Measures in or related to single transactions or movements
- Measures in or related to aggregations of transactions or movements over time
- Measures in hierarchical and other structures (parts-lists and constants)

Further division of measures to a third level can be made, if relevant, on the basis of the type of object measured.

Formal data element definition

In 1976 a major study of information systems at a Philips Division was carried out. This involved collating some hundreds of data elements, representing quantitative and financial data from many sources. Needing to define each of these data elements in some standard way for the purpose of comparison, the analysis team realized that for this very large population of data elements there are certain independent aspects which must be represented in all definitions of the population. These ideas spurred a program of study of business data elements in many type-classes so that a pattern of aspects and aspect-terms emerged. It means that for each type-class, a standard table known as a 'List of Permitted Aspect-Terms' (LOPA) is produced. Figure 7.10 shows a simplified LOPA which helps to solve the problem of defining many of the various delivery dates shown in Figure 7.11.

Aspects }	Kind of value	Subject value concept form		Status	Hole	Related concept
Aspect terms }	code description	date week	abbreviated full yww ywwd yymmdd yyddd	ordered confirmed actual	issue shipment receipt	order product

Example 'formal definition'

Code, date, ywwd, ordered, receipt, product

Corresponding possible 'user definition'

Date, coded in the form ywwd. Stated in an order, at which the customer wants to receive the goods.

Figure 7.10   'Delivery date' definition problem: simplified List Of Permitted Aspect terms (LOPA)

To define any particular data element, its type-class and then its appropriate LOPA are found. Its formal definition is then made by taking the one appropriate aspect-term from each relevant aspect from the LOPA. This string of terms is a definition expressed in a syntax which is independent of natural languages. If LOPAs and formal definitions are made in English for all data elements of interest, then it is possible:

- To derive a user description definition in ordinary English, understandable to non-experts in formal definition. The user description should be precise due to the firm basis of the formal definition.
- To translate automatically the English LOPAs and formal definitions into any other language for which there is a one-to-one translation table of the aspect terms. User descriptions in the new language can of course then be derived.
- To store the LOPAs and formal definitions in a computer (for example, in a data dictionary) so that the uniqueness of each formal definition can be checked. When a new formal definition is required, it can be checked whether new aspect-terms have to be added to the LOPA.

A LOPA is therefore an open-ended, data element standard definition generator for a given type-class.

Controlled vocabulary
Aspect-terms must be controlled not only per LOPA, but also across different LOPAs. The aspect-terms must themselves be defined and a

controlled vocabulary of permitted aspect-terms established. It is no use having a few controlled data elements using the term 'cost-price' in their formal definitions if this term is used by two groups to mean different things (homonyms) and a third group uses the term 'factory-price' for the intended concept (synonyms). Concepts expressed by homonyms must be carefully distinguished, and synonyms must be recognized in a controlled way. Building up this standard vocabulary of terms for the company is pure systems analysis work which cannot be automated. It will normally be done by the data administrator in consultation with the end users and analysts of the systems concerned.

It may be argued that the problem of data element definitions has been shifted to a problem of defining terms. This is partly true, but this problem was always present before the idea of formal definitions arose. The advantage now is that terms which may be related, or should be distinguished will now be grouped mostly under the same aspect in the LOPAs of one or more type-classes. The distinctions and relations which must be made are now easier to find.

	'Name'	Definition
1	'Required delivery period'	Date on which the customer expects the ordered goods available.
2	*'Asked delivery period'	Asked period (in weeks or months) within which goods must be sent to the customer.
3	*'Date outstanding order'	Date on which a still out-standing order on a supplier for an article code must be available for issue by the factory store.
4	*'Delivery date'	Indicates the Monday of the week in which the component must be delivered.
5	'Delivery date (despatch)'	(No definition.)
6	*'Ordered delivery date'	Date on which a particular order must be delivered According to concern calendar code.
7	'Delivery date'	Date on which a purchase order is scheduled to be delivered by a supplier.

* Collation of data elements from different libraries related to (?) 'delivery date'.

Figure 7.11   Collation of data elements related to 'delivery date'

References

1 *DB/DC Data Dictionary Planning and Design Textbook*, IBM SR20–74780–0, Sept 1982.
2 'A Systematic Approach to the Definition of Data,' C.R. Symons and P.Tijsma, *Computer Journal*, vol. 25, no. 4, 1982.

8

Documentation as an administration tool

The documentation of the database environment is a very important tool for all the participants in the operation of the database. Management depends on it for supervisory review and future planning; the data administrator depends on it for control, management, planning and maintenance; the programmers depend on it for development parameters and use; and the users depend on it for the effective use of the database system.

This section refers to documentation sets which are either wholly or partially supported by a data dictionary. Any of the sets can be supported by the data dictionary if the data administrator defines which entity types will be used to contain the documentation, and implements the design in a manner which incorporates the data dictionary as an integral partner in the design process.

Documentation produced as a result of work being done, rather than as a necessary and integral part of the work itself, has a limited range of usefulness. Program flow charts are a prime example of 'resulting documentation' that are almost invariably out of date. However, documentation produced as a natural part of the design process provides current information on the design process and its status, and a means of changing the documentation as new ideas and information impact its contents. Documentation produced as a result of work being done prevents more costly revisions and updates after the fact.

Paper dictionaries are most heavily impacted by process changes and are not as reliable as automated dictionaries. Automated dictionaries are much easier to change if the proper features are available.

8.1 Database documentation

Documentation generally provides information to be used by both the data administrator and the database administrator in designing, maintaining and controlling the database environment. Documentation provides an understanding of systems, informaton for maintenance and review and information for supervisory review. Database documentation supports the process of system design as well.

Periodic supervisory review of information assures that the database meets various needs, and that the peformance is adequate to assure both long-range and immediate performance requirements.

When personnel turnover occurs, the better the documentation the quicker a new employee becomes familiar with the product and able to perform the job. Documentation provides the source of information needed to maintain continuity in the event of the loss of experienced personnel and in training new personnel as well.

Database documentation provides communication between participants in the database environment. It provides a means of communicating information among analysts, programmers and operators about shared data resources.

Documentation specifies the standards and procedures required by internal and external sources to which the users should conform. In some cases, documentation will flag applications, procedures, or data use which do not comply with the standards specified. It monitors the data/information activity, so that the data administrator need only make decisions based upon the information supplied by the documentation.

8.2 Data dictionary supported documentation

A data dictionary is designed to support certain areas of the documentation necessary for the management and evolution of the database. These are volatile either wholly or in part, and the data dictionary immediately reflects changes in the documentation. The specific areas supported by a data dictionary are as follows:

Data element

A data dictionary generates information necessary to maintain and review activity and/or creation involving data elements by identifying all unique elements, providing a narrative description of all elements in the database and identifying all the characteristics of each data element. A data dictionary shows the format in which each element is used as well. A data dictionary describes where each element is used, showing both in which program and/or in which record the element is used. It maintains edit and validation rules governing the integrity of the elements in the database. Currently such documentation is ex post facto but the rules can be stored in an active, integrated data dictionary for immediate access. The data dictionary documentation provides security control by the creation and maintenance of passwords governing access to particular data elements.

Data record/file

The data dictionary generates information necessary to maintain and review activity and/or creation involving records and files within the database by providing a narrative description of all records and files in the database. It describes the contents of each record or file in the database. It describes the contents of each record or file including the date elements used in each, and where each record or file is used showing both in which program and/or in which system each is used. Data dictionary documentation provides the data structure of the records and/or files and the relationships between or among records and files. It also describes the use of each record or file including access keys, number or occurrences and estimated growth rate of the record or file. Data dictionary is also useful in planning the growth of the database, not just in ex post facto maintenance.

Data structure

A data dictionary generates information necessary to maintain and review the data structure within the database. Data dictionary identifies the file structure, describes the interrelationships of the data at various levels and maintains the area considerations of the database.

General text

A data dictionary allows for unlimited textual information to be associated with an entity occurrence of any type. This means that the documentation of the item can be maintained directly with the item in the dictionary and modified or reported as necessary.

8.3 Analysis/maintenance documentation

The data dictionary can be used to document activity so that any proposed changes or additions to the database system can be pre-tested to determine their total impact. Documentation, either wholly or partially supported by a data dictionary, will monitor the following database areas.

Transaction

Formatted screens are used to develop information for transactions that are unique to the company, yet are within data dictionary parameters. In other words, user-defined transactions are put on a formatted screen that automatically inputs to data dictionary. The transaction then becomes a part of the transaction matrix, and the data administrator is assured of the transaction's reflection of specified standards for procedures. In monitoring the user-defined transactions, database documentation describes the transaction, the contents of the transaction including the files and elements used and the function of the transaction. It describes the processing mode in which the transaction takes place and estimates the volume and frequency of each transaction as well.

Data element/file reference

The documentation of the database provides the information necessary for referencing elements to the files in which they reside and for referencing the files to the elements contained within them. To maintain this reference information, database documentation describes the file contents including the data elements in each file and the common application of each file and element. It provides user cross references for review, monitoring and easy access to files and elements.

Data element/application (reference)

The database documentation provides the information necessary for referencing elements to the application and/or the user that uses the element and vice versa. The documentation describes the application cross-references to the user and to the elements necessary, and describes the user functions for each application and element. It describes the desired responses for the application and the user also.

The database documentation is vital to the system development life-cycle to determine how costly and/or how beneficial an addition or extension to any part of the system will be *Before* it is initiated.

8.4 Application system documentation

The major objective of the application system documentation is to fully describe the requirements of a specific system in sufficient detail to permit programming to reflect those requirements. The specifications for application system documentation are prepared by the systems analyst in coordination with the user and the data administrator. The systems analyst determines what functions and information are necessary for the programmers to reflect user needs, and the data administrator in conjunction with the database administrator determine what is possible and/or feasible within the confines of the database environment.

The contents of the application system documentation are wholly supported by a data dictionary. This manages and maintains the information necessary for documentation to reflect changing user requirements and systems design. The data dictionary:

- States the purpose of the application system and the system's objective in a narrative form.
- Provides a descriptive narrative of the functions of the system.
- Identifies the outputs of the system and describes the format of the output.

- Describes the process logic of the system.
- Describes the input for the system and outlines the methods of input.
- Provides a cross-reference of the application system use. (This is augmented and reviewed by the database administrator). The application system documentation provides a cross-reference for data elements, data files and data structure (either area or database sub-set).

8.5 Program documentation

The major objective of program documentation is to provide a complete set of information concerning an application program in an operating environment. The contents of the program documentation are, in part, supported by a data dictionary, in that it allows source programs to be changed and the changes to be reflected almost immediately. There should be a very close liaison between the data dictionary and the source management library system. Copybooks for access to the database should be automatically generated from the dictionary, and updates to the source library management system should be reflected automatically in the data dictionary. Whether it is automated or non-automated, program documentation:

- Provides a narrative description of the systems objective.
- Provides a narrative description of the function of each program.
- Describes the input/output formats for each program and the distribution of the inputs and outputs.
- Describes the processing logic of the programs and the rules governing that processing.
- Provides program listings showing each program, its function and its application.
- Describes the operating procedures for each program.
- Provides referencing for the status code of each program.
- Describes the user procedures applicable to each program.
- Describes the timing requirements of each of the programs.
- Lists the authorization specifics for each program.

The program documentation for a database management system provides the program's view of the date structure. This helps the database administrator and the user perform maintenance to increase response time and further tune the programs or data organization. The documentation of the program view of the data structure helps the data administrator to control evolution within the system development life-cycle as well as by aiding evolution conformity to the existing data structure and by helping in the determination of the standards and guidelines of the cycle itself.

The database program documentation demonstrates whether or not a certain program logic is database structure-dependent. For example, if the program logic is dependent upon the database structure, any changes or additions made to the program that would in any way effect that processing logic would have to reflect the standards for procedure governed by that structure.

8.6 Operations function documentation

The operations function documentation is critical to the cost- and time-effective use of a database environment because it lets the operators know what procedures are available and how each impacts all other operations within the database. The database administrator has a critical responsibility to see to it that updates to all operations function documentation are done promptly and correctly to avoid negative impact on the effective operation of the database.

The back-up, restart and recovery procedures for database management system are documented in the operations function documentation including information for periodic database dump, transaction logs and checkpoint pauses.

The scheduling of processing guidelines are contained in the operations function documentation as well. The scheduling depends on the mode of processing and the resources at hand, but the database administrator thoroughly analyses both and sets the guidelines well before the processing begins in the database. The analysis includes on-line, batch, or dual processing, on-line database sharing and priority scheduling.

8.7 Database management system documentation

The vendor-supplied documentation provides the information necessary to operate the database system effectively. Nevertheless, the vendor cannot be totally specific for every installation. Therefore, the data administrator may want to provide selected supplements or documents for company-specific information. Company specific supplements could include specific procedures for recovery, operator instruction, scheduling requirements and so on.

The database administrator should define, document and distribute all the specific procedures for the use of database management system and other products used in conjunction with the database. The database administrator may choose to provide some 'security by ignorance' measures. By withholding certain documents or sections of documents from specific users, the database administrator somewhat controls what the users can and cannot do by not providing them with the instructions on how to do certain tasks. The database administrator also sees to it that those updates are applied to all documents so that all the documentation in the company is current.

8.8 Database management system command code documentation

The database management system command code documentation provides the application programmer with the procedures required to use the software. Standards for usage of the commands are the syntactical protocol of database activity, the sequence of calls and the buffer organization that allow the database to perform efficiently.

If the command codes are defined in data dictionary in the same way as user-defined entities are, it will maintain those usage standards, the definitions of the command codes and the source code dynamically. The programmer can call these standards from data dictionary into the source library interface and use an 'INCLUDE' statement in the program to access the interface. This makes maintenance of the programs easier because any modifications of the commands, codes or standards of usage are made only to the data dictionary and are immediately transparent to the program.

Because the source code is also put into the source library from data dictionary as a member interface, any changes in the source code are made in one place, at one time and they are immediately transparent to all programs via that interface.

The database management system command code documentation contains necessary information for the programmers to use when developing application programs because it:

- Provides each command name
- Defines each command and describes its meaning
- Provides the call format
- Describes the use of each command including
  1) pre-requisite actions
  2) process narrative
  3) status conditions
- Comments on any irregularities or any other factors of usage about the command codes which require further explanation.

9

Privacy, security and integrity

The issues of privacy, security, and integrity within the database environment are important in database design, performance and maintenance. Privacy, security, and integrity are all closely related concepts, but, in fact, the differences among the three are substantial as far as the role played by the data administrator and the database administrator are concerned. The specific definition of each of the concepts are as follows:

Privacy – the right of individuals or institutions to control the collection and dissemination of personal information.

Security – the protection of the computer resources from accidental or intentional destruction, modification, or disclosure.

Integrity – the correctness, accuracy, and timeliness of data within a certain level of appropriateness.

The data administrator and the database administrator are responsible for the privacy, security, and integrity within the database environment including all data and processing. Security of the database includes the protection of data from deliberate or inadvertent disclosure, modification, or destruction. System integrity is the consistency, completeness, adherence to specifications, freedom from intrusion, and predictability of a system.

9.1 Computer security issues

One might ask at this point, 'Why do we need security?' The answer is not a simple one. One of the primary reasons is the growing realization that data is an asset of a company. Because computer professionals have done such a good job of establishing computer resources in the business environment, many businesses today would not survive beyond a week to ten days if they could not process their data. For example, imagine how long a bank or department store would stay in business without its computerized data or the ability to process it.

Many years ago when data processing was a purely 'batch' process, security and control were implemented through external, physical measures. The exposure was low because much of a company's vital information was not stored on the computer. As data processing has matured, lmost all of a company's data has moved to the computer. Storage of all records on computers means that highly sensitive information about company planning strategies or personnel is now stored electronically rather than in someone's locked filing cabinet.

As we make advances in computing technology, the exposures associated with potential loss of integrity in our computing environment also increases. The development of large, shared databases, increased ability to access this data on-line, and the proliferation of remote terminals all contribute to increased risk. Moreover, access via remote terminals is no longer restricted to computing professionals. For instance, consider the growth of automated teller machines, point-of-sale terminals, grocery checkout scanners and the increased use of electronic transfer of funds, all of which have directly affected the general public.

This increased impact of computers on the general public has also enhanced public awareness of security issues. The public is rapidly becoming aware that the data is not owned by the bank or the credit service bureau, but that the data is really theirs. So the need for accuracy and integrity of data is coming closer to home for the general public. Anyone who has ever had a personal loan request refused because of information supplied by one of the many credit agencies has certainly felt the impact of the need for data accuracy.

Another item of increased public awareness is the publication from time to time, of incidents of the use of computers to perpetrate fraud or embezzle money. While only the largest cases receive widespread notoriety, each insurance funding scandal or misappropriation of funds through the misuse of computers plants yet another seed of doubt in the mind of the public.

The last, and perhaps most important, incentive for the establishment of computing security is the increased interest by legislative bodies in accounting controls and individual privacy. Legislation is in force now in the following countries:

- USA
- France
- West Germany
- Sweden
- Canada
- United Kingdom

The UK Data Protection Act

The pressure for data protection legislation in the UK has been slow to develop, but has been continuous from the appointment of the Younger committee in 1970. The landmarks in the UK, are the Lindrop report in 1978 and the present Act, expected to be fully implemented by the spring of 1988. The stated aims of the government are to comply with overseas legislation and guidelines (in particular those of the OECD and the EEC Convention), in order that, as a major trading nation, the UK does not meet problems with respect to her trade. The Act calls for action to be taken in three main areas:

- Within the data processing department, a definition that must cover micro-computers, some aspects of word processors, micro-film systems, voice and telex systems, and with all software and applications involving 'living persons'.
- Within the personnel area, to deal responsibly and sympathetically with those who wish to question the data held about them.
- Within the management of the organization, to deal with the financial and legal implications of data protection legislation.

In addition the register of systems calls for a 'nominated person', whose name is to be published, and to whom all requests for information are to be directed.

The Act lays a number of duties upon any organization using computerized data:

- *Collection of personal data* – information has to be obtained lawfully and fairly. The sources of the information have to be disclosed.
- *Purpose* – personal data can be held only for one or more specified and lawful purposes.
- *Relevance and accuracy* – when data is being processed all relevant material is to be included and all irrelevant material is to be excluded. The data must also be up-to-date.
- *Identification of subject* – it will be unlawful to keep data in name-linked form longer than necessary.
- *Security* – there will be a legal duty to provide security against unauthorized access, or unauthorized or accidental alteration of the data.
- *Publicity* – this is through the register.
- *Rights of employees* – a data subject will have the right of access to data held about him.

9.2 Risk analysis

The data administrator and the database administrator should consider all possible contingencies which might affect the privacy, security, or integrity of any part of the database environment. To plan for the privacy, security, and integrity of data, the database administrator performs a risk analysis and sensitivity analysis and then proposes possible counter-measures for protection of the data.

The first assumption in analysing the risk factors relative to data is that there is always a risk involved in any processing. It is also assumed that all risks cannot be eliminated no matter what preventative measures are taken. Therefore, the data administrator analyses the data to assess the levels of risk and the degree of probability involved in the risk. The data administrator then establishes trade-offs for protection.

It is not advisable to spend a great deal of time and money protecting low-risk data, and consequently, provide inadequate protection for high-risk data. In other words, the measures for protection should not exceed the need for protection. For example, data that is accessible to many users requires more protection than less accessible data because the risk factor is higher. Data that is more vulnerable, no matter what the cause of its vulnerability, requires a higher degree of protection than less vulnerable data. By basing protection procedures on the risks relative to data, the data administrator establishes procedures that are adequate to protect the data, yet are not too expensive or too elaborate for the needs.

Kinds of data

The first step on the risk analysis is to analyse the kinds or categories of data subject to risk. For example, database systems in a business environment have roughly the following categories of data with their relative risks:

- *Product data* – high-risk if the information is disclosed either deliberately or inadvertently.
- *Customer/supplier data* – medium-risk should the competition gain access to the information.
- *Financial data* – high-risk should the confidential financial data of the company be disclosed.
- *Personnel/personal data* – medium- to high-risk with possible legal problems should private or personal information about any personnel be disclosed either deliberately or inadvertently.
- *Strategic and tactical data* – high-risk if unauthorized people know company plans before they are complete.

The data administrator decides how to protect the information in the database, on the basis of the risk factors and decides whether to protect all the information in each category or just the highly sensitive data. For instance, those parts of the personnel files that are considered personal, such as salary information, health records, job records, and so on, should be guarded more closely than other less personal information such as addresses.

Categories of data within the database may differ from one type of organization to another. A government database system, for example, would have data categories such as the following:

- Military/defence data
- Personal data
- Survey/statistical data
- Criminal/judiciary data
- Financial/budget data

A data administrator in charge of a government database has somewhat different criteria upon which to base the risk factors relative to the data. Some governmental data is required by law to be accessible to the public, and some data is 'top secret' as a matter of national security. The data administrator, of any installation, should be aware of both internal and external rules governing the risk factors relative to the data in the database(s).

Types of risk
The data administrator analyses the types of risk. The most common types of risk are as follows:

- *Environmental* – acts of God, fire, damage to a disc, and electrical problems such as power surges.
- *Mechanical failure* – head crashes and system outages.
- *Operator errors* – human errors such as mounting the wrong tapes, failure to produce adequate back-up tapes.
- *Program error* – bugs in a program or system even if thoroughly tested and running programs.
- *Theft and fraud* – hard to detect and the damage is difficult to recover from because frequently it is not detected right away.
- *Sabotage* – a rare happening and hard to prove, but the damage is difficult to recover from.

The data administrator compares each of these types of risk with the categories of data in the particular installation to determine the probability of damage to or loss of that data. Approximately 95 per cent of all risk occurs in the first four categories.

Risk factors
In addition to analysing the types of risk, the data administrator considers the actions that relate to each type of risk. The actions relating to risk are as follows:

- *Accidental* – clearly 85 per cent of all damage to or loss of data is inadvertent and hard to avoid or foresee.
- *Deliberate passive* – inadvertent disclosure of information or damage to data is less likely to occur, but should be guarded against.

- *Deliberate active* – the consequences of premeditated disclosure of information are serious and should be considered in devising security measures.

The data administrator thus determines all the ways data can be damaged or lost, and how the damage can be accomplished before proposing methods to prevent it from happening.

9.3 Sensitivity analysis

The sensitivity of the data in each category should be evaluated to ascertain the level and expenditure that is justified for security and protection. The data administrator provides a set of conditionals for every file to determine the impact of loss or disclosure for all types of data in that file. Though there is an element of risk to all the data in the database, the risk may be low enough that it is advisable to take that risk in order to protect other data that is more highly sensitive.

Sensitivity is a function of a number of variables which must be considered before implementing any specific counter-measures to prevent loss or damage. The variables which constitute sensitivity are as follows:

- *Quantity of data* – the more the data, the harder it is to protect.
- *Quality of data* – the more critical the data, the more significant is the impact of any change or loss.
- *Degree of associability* – the ease or difficulty of connecting one type of data to another to produce potentially sensitive information dictates the significance of any disclosure or loss.
- *Degree of interpretation* – the ease or difficulty of unauthorized interpretation of information in storage dictates the level of protection necessary.
- *Age of the data* – as a rule, older data is less sensitive than current data except when it can be related to another type of data to produce a potentially sensitive result.
- *Data content* – the contents of the data dictate their sensitivity.

9.4 Types of counter-measures

The data administrator decides on the counter-measures to protect the security, privacy and integrity of the data on the basis of the risk analysis and sensitivity analysis. Some of the counter-measures available are as follows:

- *Access control* – assigning passwords or other controls to limit the access to certain data.

- *Encryption* – encrypting data to limit the ability to interpret it. Keeping in mind the level of risk and the cost of protection, the data administrator may choose to encrypt only part of the records rather than all of them.
- *File design* – protecting data by physically separating files or by partitioning the database over several devices to protect it from total destruction through such disasters as head crashes. File design can also separate records to prevent the unauthorized access to private information.
- *Hardware/software techniques* – using several methods of protection through the manipulation of hardware/software such as establishing audit trails for recoverability or establishing filter points to aid in backward processing traceable to those points.
- *Reliability/auditability* – establishing regular audit schedules of the data to make sure that it is in a state of integrity. This is a type of administrative back-up.
- *General security procedures* – monitoring the use of the data to flag any security breaches and to deter anyone from unauthorized use of the data. Establishing retaliation such as criminal or civil prosecution for violation of privacy and/or security of the data.

The data administrator selectively establishes these or other counter-measures on the basis of necessity and cost-effectiveness.

9.5 Implementation of protection procedures

In planning for the overall data security in the database environment, the data administrator should perform the following tasks:

- Identify the sources of data to protect it before it is input and eliminate some more costly integrity controls after the data is stored in the database.
- Control data conversion at all stages to protect integrity not only at the source but at various checkpoints as the database changes and grows.
- Establish edit and validation procedures to assure the integrity of the data before it goes into storage.
- Define the data to be secured, especially sensitive and irreplaceable data, to determine what cannot be recreated and provide extensive counter-measures to prevent the loss of that data.
- Establish access rights to prevent unauthorized access to data under protection. These rights generally are automated, but should be monitored and controlled by the database administrator on behalf of the data administrator. Some access controls include:
  1) *Identification control*
     – user ID (password)

         – terminal ID
         – data set ID
     2) *Functional control at the file and element levels*
         – update
         – access
     3) *Security by data content*

- Establish data storage security to make sure that the storage is physically secure both on the storage device and at the location of storage, however physically remote that location may be.
- Identify transactions and how they affect data accuracy by specifying procedures for the performance of additions, modifications and updates.
- Control data output to prevent deliberate or inadvertent interpretation of terminal displays (possibly the weakest link in security).
- Provide transmission control with encryption or coding to protect data from being intercepted in understandable form when information is transmitted from one point to another.

The objective of the data administrator is to prevent sensitive data from being damaged or lost in the first place so that time-consuming recovery is not necessary.

Depending on the type of damage done and the source of the damage, the data administrator can exercise the proper options for recovery without unnecessary expense or downtime. Some options to prevent damage from occurring or to facilitate recovery are as follows:

- *Necessary back-up* – real time or on-line processing is particularly hard to back up, but all processing should be backed up on a regular basis to provide some starting point for recovery. Back-up in the following areas is recommended:
  1) *Source data* – the original data should be kept, particularly in an interactive or on-line system
  2) *Transaction recording at the Tp monitor level* – the transactions themselves are backed up as a reference point for the recovery or for the checking of integrity
  3) *Duplicate files* – the files are periodically copied either wholly or in part to assure that a stable state of data integrity can be re-established.
- *Use of checkpoint/restart facility* – providing checkpoints periodically during all processing makes spotting erosion easier and prevents major damage or destruction from occurring.

The data administrator sees to it that data is always available, correct, and timely for the users. Therefore, the database administrator should be able to recognize a failure in processing, pinpoint the point of failure, and conduct audits with the data administrator on a regular basis. Closely monitoring the database performance to prevent erosion and minor damage helps limit recovery to catastrophic loss or destruction.

9.6 Recovery procedures for database operations

The most important factor to the recovery of the data in the database is that all recovery procedures be preplanned. The first step in planning recovery is to anticipate the possible ways destruction or damage can occur. Some of the possible sources of damage or destruction are hardware failure, software failure, human misuse, and environmental destruction. Depending on the severity of the damage, the database can be rendered:

- *Unusable* – major disasters such as complete file destruction
- 'Nearly' correct and usable – minor damage where errors are known and consistent
- *Eroded* – damage that is not recognized immediately and extent of the damage is not readily known

After determining the kinds of destruction and/or damage that can occur the data administrator and the database administrator must analyse the recovery procedures necessary to get the data back.

Factors of recovery analysis

In planning for recovery within the database, the two administrators must analyse the factors relative to the recovery procedure itself; such as:

- *Acceptable downtime* – the data administrator should determine how long the information and/or the users can tolerate downtime. This has to be done on an application basis or a user by user basis.
- *Physical size of the database* – the larger the database, the harder it is to backup. Therefore the database administrator may want to establish staged back up or recovery procedures to decrease downtime and continuous CPU time.
- *Problem classification* – the database administrator should accurately classify the problems causing damage and/or loss in order to clarify the recovery procedures and report back to the data administrator any changes necessary to them.
- *Processing environment* – the mode of processing should be considered in determining the type of recovery procedure that is most cost-effective and efficient. For example:
  1) *Batch* – easier to back up due to sheduled processing capabilities
  2) *On-line* – harder to backup because of real time processing and the hardship of down time
  3) *Both* – separate recovery procedures are needed to adequately back up both processing modes

Recovery procedures

Knowing the type of damage that can occur to data, the sensitivity of the data and the factors relative to the recovery procedure, the data administrator devises the overall recovery plan for the organization.

The database administrator has several recovery procedures to choose from to develop the recovery plan, including back-up (single or multiple physical sites, tapes, or machines) and utilities, provided by the particular database management system in use at the site.

9.7 Editing and validation as a deterrent

The first level of control for data protection is at the data capture stage. The data administrator establishes the standards for checking the quality of the data at the capture stage. The database administrator produces editing and validation rules during database and application design, so as to provide the checks to ensure the quality of all the data input or processed.

In many cases the database management system cannot provide the quality checks itself, so edit and validation is a function of the programs. The database administrator writes link routines, in accordance with the standards laid down by the data administrator, that are processed with every program to assure the consistency and the standardization of the data and processing. Some of the checks performed for edit and validation are:

- Range check on calculations to ensure their accuracy
- Checks on the field size to validate the transaction and overflow accuracy
- Data content checks to make sure the data is not only valid but correct as well
- Checks on the presence of the data to make sure that it is there
- Batch total checks to assure accuracy at any particular point in the processing

The edit and validation procedures allow continuous monitoring of data integrity to prevent inconsistencies in data accuracy.

Statistical analysis of errors

The data administrator and database administrator periodically should perform a statistical analysis of the edit and validation errors. This allows modification and improvement of those procedures without compromising the on-going protection they provide. The statistical analysis of the edit and validation procedures include analysis by type of error and the source of data input. This analysis allows the data administrator to pinpoint the sources of the errors and eliminate them before erosion occurs in the database.

Data checking

Independent data checking should be applied as close to the source of data capture as possible, especially in on-line and real-time environments. It protects data conversion and prevents erosion. There are two main tools, useful in checking independent data as close to the source of data capture as possible:

- *Intelligent terminals* – making use of all the hardware and software capabilities with terminals that are programmed to flag data that is incorrect while the data is being input
- *Masking facility* – using routines that establish integrity as data is being input before it is stored in the database.

Dependent data checking must be applied in conjunction with database access to ensure the proper value and format of the data. These dependent higher-level checks are performed by two important tools:

- *Application programs*   link edit routines that establish data value and format consistency before database introduction
- *Database management system routines* – flag data with improper value or format before introduction into database storage

By checking data before storage in the database a valuable deterrent to data erosion is provided and the number of recovery stages necessary is reduced.

10

Interface with the data administration office

To make the expectations of database technology, in terms of productivity gains and data integration that management has held, one needs to answer the problems – managerial, technical and political. Eight major problems typically arise in a database project.

- Uncommitted management
- Insufficient end-user involvement
- Lack of requirements definition
- Antiquated end-user procedures
- Lack of development discipline
- Resistance to sharing data
- Lack of data standards
- Inappropriate database management system tool

These problems can be grouped into three categories:

- Management
- End user
- Technical

DP departments, with adequate training, can normally resolve the technical problems. When it comes to the end-user and management issues, however, DP departments are at a disadvantage. In order to rectify this situation, organizations that use a database management system have to create a new function called data administration. The object of this function is to manage data as a corporate resource. It has to be organized so that it is possible to address important end-user and management issues. The new group provides the focal point for all the interfacing and communication between users and the DP department required during the planning and development stages of database system projects.

The data administration office should as liaison between corporate management, end users, and the DP department. Its mandate is to translate business plans into data resource plans. The main techniques available to do this are business modelling and data modelling. In the process, the office evaluates users' needs, weighs them against the

long-term data resource development objectives, asks DP experts for
their assessment, and then assigns individual priorities.

Figure 10.1 shows the areas within a company that interact with the
data administrations office and the type of interactions involved.

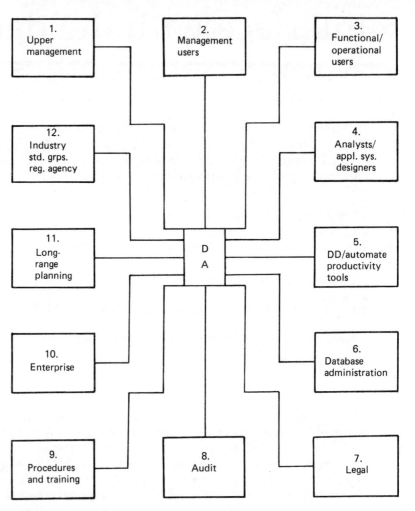

Figure 10.1　Interaction with data administration

10.1　Interface with upper management

In this area, the data administration office is involved in planning and
policy review tasks, such as:

● Reports on data management activities, including cost/benefit
analyses

- Long-range plan for information systems development
- Proposals for data standards development
- Proposals for realignment of duties or responsibilities for purposes of data security or integrity

10.2 Interface with top functional management

With this area, the data administration office is involved in operational data needs for:

- Strategic data planning
- Data resource use and management
- Cost accounting

10.3 Interface with information users

Just as with involvement with top functional management, the data administration office is involved in the operational data needs, but in this case at a more detailed level of task such as:

- Fostering data sharing in the company
- Facilitating an understanding of the relevant aspects of the data resource of the company
- Developing mutually acceptable naming conventions and data definition standards
- Satisfying user requests according to the laid down rules of the company

10.4 Interface with systems analysts and systems designers

In this area, the data administrators office is involved in the main in the requirements for new or amended data to satisfy the new application systems needs, such as:

- New query frequencies
- Tighter response times or reporting frequencies
- Different input/output media
- New policies

There are three other tasks where involvement between the analysts, designers and the data administrations offices takes place:

- Conversion of existing systems
- Information resource planning
- Service analysis

10.5 Relationship with database administration

Depending on the way a company has decided to set up the data administration office to include or not the database administrator, this relationship is either part of the internal structure of the office or a liaison with a separate technical group. In section 1, the definitions of the two functions were outlined. In section 2, checklists for typical responsibilities of the two functions were laid down. If we now summarize what was talked about in these sections, the relationship between data administration and database administration is in terms of reports and briefing on the moving of the database administrator's execution of data administrator's policy in:

- General database and data dictionary performance
- Systems security and privacy safeguards
- Mapping from a conceptual model into a physical database design
- Adherence to data naming conventions
- Control of access to data dictionary
- Usage of data dictionary and user satisfaction with it

10.6 Interface with legal counsel

With the impact of data protection/privacy legislation this interface has become extremely vital. The rules for the use and availability of the data resource must be in place before any solutions to problems created by legislative action can be dealt with.

10.7 Interface with audit (internal/external)

Let us first look at this from the point of view of internal audit. In many companies, an internal audit department is used to vet systems before they go live. The introduction of a data administrations office leads to the following points of mutual interest:

- Providing independent assurance to management that an application system accurately and reliably accomplishes its objective
- Ensuring the inclusion of program functions and related procedures designed to check and control data preparations and processing
- Establishing continuous review and appraisal of the accuracy, reliability and quality of corporate information systems

In terms of external auditors, the data administrations office will become the major point of contact, for it is here that knowledge of the company's data lies.

10.8 Interface with company training department

If an organization has its own company training department, then the data administration office should put together a *short* presentation on the importance of data to be used as part of the induction of all employees. Obviously for new employees involved in DP or management informations departments, there has to be a more detailed follow-up course, giving details on:

- Procedures
- Standards
- Database management systems
- Data dictionary usage

10.9 Interface with industry standard groups and regulatory agencies

It is important to look outside of one's own organization. Firstly, because you will find that you are not alone in having to deal with the problems you encounter as a data administrator. Secondly, you may find that you can effect the introduction of any industry-wide data standards.

Appendices

Appendix A
Sample data administration management objectives

Sample data administration department management objectives

(Initial start-up year)

Assumption: Database administration is under data administration

Prepared for XYZ Company PLC

Data administration department objectives

Expected results	*Performance measures*
1 Set up and maintain the data administration function as an integral part of XYZ Company.	1a Develop the data administration charter. • Charter is approved by both the management counterpart committee and upper management by NNNN quarter, 198N. 1b Define data administration departmental job descriptions. • Both MIS upper management and the personnel department approve the job description by NNNN quarter, 198N. 1c Establish formalized working relationships with other MIS departments. • The data administration function is both consulted and utilized by other organizations throughout XYZ Company. 1d Present data administration and database technology concepts to both data processing and end-user personnel. • Documents are periodically distributed by data administration to promote a better understanding of the concepts of database and data administration. • Presentations are made to various XYZ Company organizations on selected topics. 1e Maintain contacts with other organizations which have a working data administration function for the purpose trading ideas and enhancing our own data administration function.

Expected results	*Performance measures*
	• MIS management periodically receives recommendations for further enhancing the Data Administration function
2 Manage subordinates.	2a Ongoing.
	• Data administration personnel are performing their defined jobs in an acceptable and timely manner.
3 Guide the development and enhancement of a stable database environment which is needed to support various application development projects.	3a Define the initial software tools and procedures necessary for supporting a working database environment.
	• Database procedures for supporting the creation, back-up, recovery and reorganization of database data are developed and used.
	• Additional database software is installed, tested and effectively used.
	• Standards, policies and procedures for defining, documenting and establishing new and modified database are developed and used.
	3b Gain a working knowledge of the current data environment.
	• New data requirements are documented via the data dictionary.
	• Data administration plays an active role in guiding the development of new databases.
	3c Develop an initial set of database standards, policies and procedures.
	• Standards, policies, and procedures are introduced and approved: resulting in a more responsive database environment.
4 Integrate the data administration function into the application development	4a Define data administration's roles for a database application development and implementation.

Expected results

process for the purpose of providing expertise and productive support in developing and implementing database-related applications.

5   Develop and enhance the data dictionary environment for documenting and controlling enterprise-wide data/information.

6   Help train MIS personnel in understanding and properly using database technology.

Performance measures

• Specific data administration roles are defined, documented and exercised in conjunction with the accepted application development life-cycle methodology.

5a   Establish a stable data dictionary environment to be used for documenting and controlling, retrieving and reporting information about data.
• Procedures and standards for documenting fields (data items) are finalized and used within the NNNN quarter, 198N.
• Procedures are in place for initiating and controlling database documenting and maintaining both live and development databases by NNNN quarter, 198N.

6a   Work with the training department in helping to develop database training programs.
• A basic database curriculum relative to Company XYZ is defined by NNNN quarter, 198N.
• Database products are being used properly by NNNN quarter, 198N.

Appendix B
Data administration sample implementation plan

Data administration department sample implementation plan

198X

Prepared by: Manager, data administration

Assumption: database administration reports to data administration

Synopsis

I. Purpose

II. Scope
- General considerations
- Establishing a stable database environment

III. Key assumptions/inhibitors
- Key assumptions
- Key inhibitors

IV. Establish a stable database environment
- Develop standards, guidelines, policies, and procedures
- Database environment familiarization and support considerations
- Identify and define additional software tools and procedures

V. Integrate data administration into the application development process
- Define data administration roles

VI. Establish a working data dictionary environment
- Objectives
- General considerations
- Data dictionary task list

VII. Develop database training program development
- Responsibilities
- General considerations
- Course selections

VIII. Provide ongoing project support for application development
- Objectives
- Tasks

IX. Data planning approaches/considerations
- Overview
- Objectives
- Benefits
- Considerations

I. Purpose

The purpose of this 198X data administration plan is to define the requirements which are necessary for successfully implementing a workable and productive data administration function. This plan represents a statement of intent and commitment that our organization is willing to recognize that data is a corporate resource which must be carefully managed as with any other key corporate asset (for example, cash).

II. Scope

This data administration implementation plan identifies what has to be accomplished for successfully implementing a workable and productive data administration function. Specific areas to be addressed by this plan include:

General considerations

- Confirming the data administration charter of responsibilities as a working document.
- Establishing data administration job descriptions.
- Communicating database and data resource management concepts via presentations and written documents.
- Continually upgrading our data administration environment through ideas, gained by visiting other companies, and attendance at various user group meetings/seminars.

Establishing a stable database environment

- Identifying, developing and/or acquiring standards, guidelines, policies, and procedures as they relate to data administration activities and the database management system.
- Gaining a working knowledge of our application database environment and providing the necessary data administration support.
- Defining database – related software tools and procedures.
- Recommending and acquiring additional database software tools.
- Integrating the data administration function into the application development and maintenance process by defining specific tasks to be performed.
- Defining, developing and implementing a working data dictionary environment for documenting and controlling corporate data/information.
- Helping develop a database curriculum relative to the (organization) environment in conjunction with the training department.
- Providing data administration support for the various existing application projects as well as other identified projects.

- Evaluating data planning approaches for helping to establish a stable data environment.

III. Key assumptions/inhibitors

Key assumptions

- There is a strong and active management commitment to support the efforts identified in this plan.
- The recognition that data is a corporate resource which must be carefully managed and controlled via the data administration function.
- Data administration will actively participate in the project planning and provide specific support roles for application development activities.
- Specific standards, guidelines, policies and procedures will be established by data administration for stabilizing our data environment.

Key inhibitors

- Priority changes initiated by management could possibly impact the ability to complete tasks specified by this plan.
- The inability to recognize that the data administration department and database technology will gradually evolve over years through steady, dedicated efforts and accomplishments.
- The inability to recognize data as a corporate asset would result in treating database as an access method rather than as a methodology for managing a corporate resource.

IV. Establish a stable database environment

Develop standards, guidelines, policies and procedures

Overview
Develop and/or acquire standards, guidelines, policies and procedures pertaining to data administration and the database management system.

Data administration related

- *Data element naming*
  COBOL data element naming standard.
  COBOL data element naming procedure.
- *Other identified procedures for:*

Data elements documentation.
Database design as it relates to:
– Data analysis requirements
– Logical database design
– Physical database design.

Database management system related
- Naming standards
- Database documentation requirements relating to:
Databases, areas, files and so on
Database creation and modification
Database back-up and recovery
Database reorganization.

Database environment familiarization and support considerations

- **Document programs, transactions, databases, data elements, and other entities via the data dictionary.**
  - Establish meaningful dictionary entity relationships and implementing automated impact analysis capabilities. The data dictionary can be used to answer questions such as:
    'Determine what processes are affected by adding new data elements to a particular database.'
  - Control all database related changes via the data dictionary.

Identify and define additional software tools and procedures

- Justify new database – related software.
  – Budgeted
  – Non-budgeted (198X projections)
- Justify, test and use each newly installed database software using the following procedures:
  Step 1: Request software installation data from technical support via memo.
  Step 2: Rejustify budgeted software via a memo sent to the approving director.
  Step 3: Upon approval, request operations to order approved software to coincide with the planned installation date.
  Step 4: Test new software product after installation.
  Step 5: Begin using software on a regular basis.
- Establish a data analyst workbench of database software tools and procedures (database space estimations) to provide better support for problem resolution and problem prevention.
- Develop database diaries reflecting all relevant information and activities pertaining to each database file

- Evaluate prototyping databases using a fourth-generation tool as a productivity approach for developing applications.
- Develop additional database software verification procedures for ensuring the successful installation and transitions to new releases and periodic software modifications

V. Integrate data administration into the application development process

Define data administration roles

- Gain a working knowledge of the application methodology being used.
- Define data administration roles throughout the application life-cycle.
- Integrate data administration roles not identified within the specific methodology phase.

VI. Establish a working data dictionary environment

Objectives

The data dictionary environment will serve several purposes:

- *Repository of data about data* – in order to administer and use database systems, careful documentation must be maintained on data names, characteristics, relationships, and so on.
- *Control mechanism* – the effective administration of data and program security requires a mechanism which will assist data administration in generating database definitions and database programs access requirements.
- *System development tool* – as system development and maintenance depend on more databases and new file structures, a responsive tool is needed to assist the analyst in documenting and controlling the development cycle.

General considerations

- Determine how best the data dictionary environment can be used to service business needs.
- Gain a working understanding of the data dictionary's capabilities.
- Develop the necessary manual and automated procedures for effectively supporting database processing and documentation.
- Identify what useful functions cannot be accomplished through the existing data dictionary facilities and determine how best to satisfy

those needs through dictionary customization, query language access, fourth-generation tool and/or report writer reports, or additional software acquisitions.
- Determine how best to enforce naming standards and other database – related standards via the data dictionary.
- Identify and project additional uses of the data dictionary. For instance, how can the data dictionary be used to support automated database design and data modelling for future efficient database/ data file development.
- Determine how best to secure the data dictionary contents and implement security and integrity (that is essential backup and recovery facilities).

Data dictionary task list

- Prototype data dictionary capabilities:
  - Generating and centrally controlling database I/O area copy book information.
  - Performing automated impact analysis using the data dictionary to determine what programs would be affected by certain database changes.
  - Determining dictionary report and query capabilities.
  - Securing the data dictionary facilities.
  - Exploring other potential uses of the data dictionary such as storing jobs, job steps, on-line transactions and data set documentation and relationships for the purpose of establishing additional, automated, impact analysis capabilities.
  - Determining the best dictionary options for our environment.
  - Establishing a stable but useful dictionary environment. For example, how long should the on-line dictionary environment be available throughout each regular working day. Also, how can we best minimize interruptions caused by both scheduled and unscheduled CPU shutdowns.
  - Evaluating how best we can tune the data dictionary environment to work more efficiently.
- Provide a central source for controlling the database management system changes. For instance:
  - Establish and control live/development database dictionary environments for initiating and staging application database changes.
  - Maintain an audit trail for database changes.
- Document all database related information including:
  - Databases, areas, files, fields, and so on.
  - Database relationships.
  - Database – related procedures for database creation, expansion, back-up and recovery, and reorganization.

- Detailed documentation profiles for each required data dictionary subjects.
- Provide proper dictionary back-up, recovery, expansion and tuning facilities.
- Develop dictionary – related standards, guidelines, policies and procedures.
- Develop dictionary software verification procedures for ensuring the successful installation and transitions to new releases and periodic software modifications.

VII. Develop database training program

Responsibilities

All efforts pertaining to database training as outlined by this plan will be initiated by data administration and thoroughly evaluated by the training department in terms of reasonability and practicality prior to any implementation.

General considerations

- Determine different approaches to database and associated software training from both an economical and practical point of view.
  - Establish a database - related reading list for various levels of interest.
  - Identify, evaluate and recommend various approaches for potential training such as:
    Video tapes
    Independent study programs
    Outside courses both through direct company registrations and consortiums
    In-house courses (either internally developed or vendor-developed and taught)
    Internally developed workshop exercises
  - Employ coaching techniques using either data administration and/or training departments.
  - Establish a periodic database newsletter and/or technical bulletin to share ideas related to good database techniques/problem resolutions.

Course selections

- Evaluate specific database training requirements based on both anticipated as well as identified needs.

VIII. Provide ongoing project support for application development

Objectives

- Provide timely and adequate support for data administration – related application development tasks.
- Minimize data administration's impact on the application being developed.
- Provide guidance in using a standard database design methodology.

Tasks

- Review current project schedules.
- Identify any additional data administration tasks
- Identify any additional database and associated software training requirements.
- Communicate intended data dictionary support
- Establish revised target dates

IX. Data planning approaches/considerations

Overview

Data planning is a top-down planning approach used to develop computer applications that have shareable data resources. This approach is identified via the following criteria:

- Data is managed as a company resource and is separated from the applications which use that data.
- Data is organized around company subjects instead of being tailored to individual application areas. This approach results in data structures which are more stable and shareable. Company subjects are identified as major classes of data and are also referred to as subject databases.
- Each information system is tailored to access whatever subject databases are necessary to serve a group of closely related business activities. These activities are supported by a company-oriented subject database environment. Such an environment is established by migrating existing systems and data files into a well planned subject database environment.

Objectives

- Promote a corporate-wide view of data and its value as an essential resource.

- Optimize the use of data by eliminating/minimizing its duplication and enhancing its integrity.
- Provide more reliable, accurate and consistent data/information resources for decision making.

Benefits

- Support multiple applications through a set of fully integratable and shareable data resources.
- Data is structured in its most stable form resulting in more effective and productive use of our data environment.
- Effective implementation of shared subject databases through data planning results in minimizing data redundancy. There is the potential to save existing DASD as you make the transition from our replicated data environment to a more efficient subject database -type environment. Also, we can experience cost avoidance through a more optimum use of future DASD resources.

Considerations

- Evaluate the possibility of initiating a system-by-system inventory of existing application data files and records and data elements. The intent would be to store this information onto the data dictionary and identify duplicate data usage.
- Develop corporate policies regarding the use and custodianship of data. This would represent an initial step for establishing data security.
- Evaluate the possibility of putting value on the data and its usage as another approach to establishing chargeback.
- Evaluate available software tools for potentially supporting a data planning effort.
- Attend a course on data planning and present findings to management.
- Arrange for an in-house presentation on data planning.

Appendix C
Sample data administration charter

Sample data administration charter for Company XYZ

Assumption: the database administration function reports to the manager of the data administration department

Synopsis

I. Purpose

II. Policy

III. Scope

IV. Goals and objectives
- Ensure the integrity of XYZ Company's data resource
- Improve the effectiveness of XYZ Company
- Ensure user requirements for information implemented; data-processing users satisfied with information

V. Responsibilities
- Strategic planning
- Design
- Controls
- Support

VI. Data administration department success factors

I. Purpose

This charter defines the responsibilities and authorities of the data administration department as they relate to the effective and efficient use of data and information throughout Company XYZ.

II. Policy

The data administration charter is based on the concept that data is an enterprise-wide resource which must be managed as any other key organizational asset, such as money and personnel. It is the policy of XYZ Company that the items defined in this charter become the basis for the scope of the responsibilities and operational authorities of the data administration department.

III. Scope

The data administration department is responsible for planning, co-ordinating, designing and managing the data resources for XYZ Company, including the software components needed to support their effective use.

The data administration department charter addresses four major areas of responsibilities:

- Strategic planning of data and data-related hardware and software.
- Design as it relates to preliminary application review, application development support and database-related design.
- Controls associated with data-related standards, guidelines and procedures; data privacy and security; the use of our data dictionary to document, manage and reference XYZ Company's information about data; and database restart/recovery, database performance monitoring and database testing and acceptance into a live database environment.
- Support of information resource/database training and education, database software and information centre activities.

IV. Goals and objectives

There are three major Data Administration goals. These goals and their associated objectives are:

Ensure the integrity of XYZ Company's data resource
Data integrity requires that Company XYZ's data be stored in an accurate, consistent and complete manner along with the mechanisms

(that is software, procedure, standards, documentation and so on) to maintain this status. The proper implementation of data integrity measures will result in reliable resources for producing information for decision making.

Specific objectives for achieving data integrity include:

- Providing the capability to precisely describe, store and retrieve information about Company XYZ's data and system resources by maintaining current, consistent, accurate, thorough and useful documentation via the data dictionary.
- Limiting data access on a need-to-know basis.
- Implementing standards and procedures relating to the storage and usage of data, especially as it relates to the standard and consistent naming of data and the specification of its attributes.
- Using the data dictionary, query language, report writer, application generator and other database management software resources for maintaining data integrity.

Improve the effectiveness and productivity of XYZ Company

Productivity and effectiveness for Company XYZ will be achieved by:

- Developing data resources which are shared and integrated within Company XYZ.
- Providing the tools and skills to access data in a timely manner.
- Delivering the necessary support for maintaining existing applications and determining new data and information requirements.
- Developing business models and data models which help define Company XYZ's business environment and determine data processing requirements to support it.

The main Data Administration objective relating to this goal is to fully co-operate with other key data processing organizations, work with key end users and contribute to the following associated objectives:

- Help provide a successful migration to a well-organized and useful database environment at Company XYZ.
- Provide the timely guidance and support for documenting, generating and successfully implementing modifications pertaining to data and their associated computer applications via the Data Dictionary.

Ensure user requirements for information implemented; data-processing users satisfied with information

It is important to ensure that user requirements for information are being implemented and that Company XYZ's data processing users are satisfied with the information being provided.

Data administration will achieve this goal by:

- Understanding Company XYZ's mission and determining the best way to support it.

- Gaining a working knowledge of Company XYZ's business.
- Helping determine data requirements to satisfy Company XYZ's informational needs by acting as a liaison between the end user and the MIS organization.
- Organizing data in the optimal fashion through clearly defined database design techniques which result in the development and use of shared data.

V. Responsibilities

The data administration department is primarily a service organization which provides support to Company XYZ's end users and other departments within data processing.

Strategic planning

Data planning
Data administration has joint responsibility with the DP development group to plan the orderly transition to a database environment by guiding the use of common data by multiple computer applications. Planning shared data usage will reduce data redundancy, minimize data inconsistencies and provide a uniform approach to organizing and implementing our data to satisfy our informational requirements.

Database software planning
Data administration will be responsible for maintaining an understanding of future trends in information technology (especially database technology) and report their possible impact to DP management. Data administration will recommend how best to use this technology in conjunction with Company XYZ's organizational objectives.

Hardware planning
Data administration will work with other DP groups in planning disc storage use. This responsibility includes the projection of disc storage estimates to accommodate future database developments as well as new database modifications and expansions. Data Administration will also assist in the planning and placement of database data sets onto disc to optimize database processing.

Design

Preliminary application review
Data administration will help evaluate each new application within the systems study/evaluation phase to help determine the feasibility of using database technology as well as identifying the potential for

sharing existing data. This review process will help identify initial additional hardware and software requirements and determine data administration department support for this project.

Application development support
Data administration will actively support the application development process. A separate standard will define specific data administration tasks associated with supporting an application throughout the application development process, in conjunction with the approved system development life-cycle methodology. The data administration tasks will be included in the overall project plan associated with the application to be developed.

Database design
Data administration and the project application development group will share responsibility for designing the data base content. A separate standard will define the database design methodology to be used. Basically, the application development group will determine and document end-user application requirements, and share responsibility with data administation for developing the logical database structural content. Data administration (via the database administrator function) will be responsible for completing the physical database design (for example, determining physical database file disc storage requirements and database data set placement onto disc storage).

Controls

Standards, guidelines and procedures
Data administration will be responsible for developing standards, guidelines, and procedures relating to:

- *Database content* – which addresses the standard for format and contents of the actual data contained in the database files.
- *Data definition* – which includes the naming, content definition, and description pertaining to information about data to be stored in the data dictionary of the company.
- *Data usage* – which represents all the activities in maintaining and accessing the data on a 'need-to-know' basis as well as defining end-user responsibility for the integrity of the data content.

A data administration standards committee consisting of major data processing organizational representatives will be responsible for reviewing and modifying the standards, guidelines and procedures initiated by the data administration department.

Documentation

Data administration will be responsible for defining the data-related documentation standards.

Data privacy and security

Data administration will maintain an awareness of the latest legislation that pertains to data privacy, data security and inform data processing management concerning their current and future impacts. In addition, data administration will be responsible for establishing a data security function, developing a data security policy for the company and selecting the appropriate data security software. Data-related password control will also be the responsibility of data administration.

Database restart and recovery

Data administration will develop and implement back-up and recovery procedures for all computer-held files in the company. These procedures will be thoroughly documented within the data dictionary and tested prior to turning over to computer operations for their use.

Database performance monitoring

Data administration will be jointly responsible with the systems programming and computer operations group for monitoring computer systems performance as it relates to all computer-held data files. Data administration will be responsible for tuning database files to processing efficiencies.

Testing and acceptance of databases

Data administration will participate in the testing and acceptance of new as well as modified computer/database applications. Data administration has both the responsibility and authority to accept a database application for live environment running that has followed established database standards, guidelines and procedures. Specific standards and procedures pertaining to database project acceptance will be reviewed with the application project team at the beginning of each project.

Application development will be responsible for establishing development test data in conjunction with the end users. Data administration will work with the application development team to ensure the timely development and availability of this data.

Support

Database training and education

Data administration will work closely with the training department in helping to evaluate and develop database-related internal training programmes, as well as helping to evaluate all outside database re-lated education programmes. Data administration will present or assist in presenting internal training programmes, where applicable.

Database related software support

Data administration will be responsible for initiating and controlling modifications to current database-related software. The systems pro-gramming group will install all new software and modifications. Data administration will assist the systems programming group in testing all major database-related software installations. Data administration will coordinate the introduction of all associated database software into the live environment to ensure the database integrity between software releases as well as to avoid database processing interrup-tions caused by poorly coordinated transitions to new software releases.

Information centre support

Data administration will help determine where data exists for satis-fying end-user information requests. Automated tools will be used to effectively support this process. In the future, data administration will establish and maintain an information centre function.

VI. Data administration department success factors

The successful implementation and continuing effective operation of the data administration department at Company XYZ is dependent on the following success factors:

- Complete and continual XYZ management support for the effective and efficient operation of the data administration function.
- Periodic evaluation of this charter for the purpose of upgrading its contents as data administration proves its value and accepts more responsibility in managing XYZ's data as a company resource.
- Promoting and implementing the control and optimum usage of XYZ's quality data on a 'need-to-know' basis which results in effec-tive information to be used for company decision making.
- Recognized and accepted data administration responsibility and authority to develop and implement meaningful and useful stan-dards, guidelines and procedures relating to the definition and usage of XYZ's data.
- Implementing a shared data environment that encourages the use of common and consistent data across Company XYZ's organizational boundaries with minimized and planned data redundancy.
- Sufficient data administration department staffing to continually and effectively support the responsibilities and authorities defined within this charter.

- The establishment of a data security function within the data administration department. The security function will be responsible for developing data security-related standards, policies and procedures pertaining to custodianship and usage of data at XYZ.

Appendix D
Bibliography

Books

Application Systems Development Methodologies: Solution or Problem?
D. Connor, Savant Institute, 1982

Creating and Planning the Corporate Database System Project, L. J. Cohen,
Mountain House Publishing Inc., 1981

*Concepts and Terminology for the Conceptual Schema and the Information
Base*, ISO TC97/SC5/WG3, Editor J. J. van Griethugsen

Data Administration, Burroughs Manual

Data Administration: A Practical Guide to Successful Data Management,
W. R. Durell, McGraw Hill, New York, 1985

Data Administration Guide, ADR manual DB2G–AC–00

Data Administration Methodology, Report of the Data Administration
Methodology Project, Guide, Jan. 1978

*Database Administration: Experience from a European Survey. Evaluation
and Implementation of Database Systems*, GMD, IRIA, CNR, NCC, Jan.
1980

Database Directions Information Resource Management: Strategies and Tools,
editor A. H. Goldfine, NBS Special publication 500–92, US Government Printing Office, Washington, 1982

*Data Dictionary/Directory Systems: Administration, Implementation and
Usage*, B. W. Leong-Hong and B. K. Plagman, John Wiley & Sons
Inc., 1982

Data Dictionaries and Data administration, R. R. Ross, Amacom, 1981

DB/DC Data Dictionary Planning and Design Study Guide, IBM SR20–
7478–0, Sept. 1982

DB/DC Data Dictionary Planning and Design Textbook, IBM SR20–7477–
0, July 1982

Establishing the Data Administration Function, Guide International Corp.,
1977

Establishment of a Database Administration Function, Share SSD246, 10
June 1974

Information Systems Development: A Flexible Framework, British Computer Society Information Systems Analysis and Design Working
Party Journal of Developments, editor R. Maddison, 1983–4

Managing the Data-base Environment, J. Martin, Prentice-Hall Inc., 1983

Managing the Data Resource, R. L. Nolan, West Publishing Company, 1982

Megatrends: Ten New Directions Transforming Our Lives, J. Naisbitt, Macdonald & Co, London, 1982

Strategic Data-planning Methodologies, J. Martin, Prentice-Hall, 1982

Structured Systems Analysis: Tools and Techniques, C. Gane and T. Sarson, Improved System Technologies Inc., Oct 1977

Structured System Development Techniques: Strategic Planning to System Testing, G. Collins and G. Blay, Pitman, 1982

The Database Administrator, J. K. Lyon, Wiley, 1976

The Database Administrator Today: Results of a Survey Done by Members of the Data Base Administration Project of the Data Base Division of Guide Europe, Guide, Dec. 1975

The Role of the Database Administration, NCC

Papers and articles

'A Survey of the Data Administration Function in Large Canadian Organizations? I. B. McCritick, M. Sc. thesis, University of British Columbia, Vancouver, 1971

'A Systematic and Practical Approach to the Definition of Data,' C. R. Symons and P. Tijsma, *Computer Journal*, vol. 25, No. 4, 1982

Chief Information Officer? M. Weiner & J. Girvin, *Computerworld, In Depth*, 13 May 1985

Codasyl D B C? DBA Working Group, British Computer Society report, June 1975

Data Administration in the Organization', S. Holloway, *Data Processing*, vol. 28, no. 4, May 1986.

'Data Administration vs. Data Base Administration', G. Tillman, *Infosystems*, 98–102, 2/84

'Data Administration: It's Crucial', A. D. Shah, *Datamation*, 187–192, Jan. 1984

'Database Administrator: Superman or Superseded?', M. McLening, *Datalink*, 24 Jan. 1983

'Data Administration: the Way to Make Management Aware', N. Hawker, *Datalink*, 30 July 1984

'Data Base Administration – Organization and Tasks', J. L. Weldon, NYU, Graduate School of Business Administration, Working Paper 78–143 (CA), Dec. 1978

'Data Protection Legislation in the UK', G. Morrison, Proceedings of the British Computer Society Database Specialist Group Conference, *Database 84 – Database Design Update*

'Database Administration – Classical Patterns, Some Experience and Trends', J–P De Blasis, Proceedings of National Computer Conference, 1977

'Database Control Functions', report of the British Computer Society/ CODASYL DDLC Database Administration Working Group, 1981

'Designing Data to Avoid Micro Disasters', N. Hawker, *Datalink*, 4 June 1984

'How to Triumph Over Your Pressing Problems', R. Hegarty and T. Smith, *Computer Weekly*, 24 Nov. 1983

'Information as a Corporate Asset', D. R. Vincent, *Computer world in depth*, 26 Sept. 1983

'Managing Information as a Corporate Resource', T. R. H. Sizer, *Computer Bulletin*, Sept. 1982

'Some Realities of Data Administration – a Management Briefing,' B. K. Kahn, Graduate School of Management, Boston University, Feb. 1983

'Strategies for Information Requirements Determination', G. B. Davis, *IBM Systems Journal* 21, 4–29, 1982

'The Data Administrator Function', *EDP Analyser* 11/72, vol. 10, no. 11

'The Many Faces of the DBA', E. K. Yasaki, *Datamation*, May 1977

'The People Who Matter in the Administration,' R. Hegarty and T. Smith, *Computer Weekly*, 8 Dec. 1983

'Practice of Data Base Administration', J. L. Weldman, Proceedings of National Computer Conference, 1979

'The State of Practice of Data Administration – 1981', M. L. Gillenson, Commuications of the ACM, vol. 25, no. 10, Oct. 1982

'Two Teams, One Goal', B. Rollier, *Datamation*, April 1982

'Understand and Communicate to Take Good Care of Your Data', N. Hawker, Datalink, 5 Mar. 1984

'Very Large Data Base Administration', T. H. Johnson and J–P De Blasis, Wharton School, University of Pennsylvania, 76–04–06

'What do Data Administrators Really Do?', I. B. McCrinck and R. C. Goldstein, *Datamation*, Aug 1980

'Why It Is a Good Thing to Treat Data Management with Care, R. Hegarty and T. Smith, *Computer Weekly*, 17 Nov. 1983

'Internal Papers of British Computer Society Data Administration Working Party 1982–1985